"Siang-Yang Tan is one of my heroes of the faith. He is primarily a devoted lover of Jesus who happens to be a committed psychologist among his other roles as pastor, teacher, mentor, speaker, and researcher. His love, faith, humanity, and wisdom are evident in this brief book about counseling, the Holy Spirit, and how they fit hand in glove. This is an up-to-the-minute primer on his faith and thinking."

—EVERETT L. WORTHINGTON JR.
Virginia Commonwealth University, emeritus

"This is a brilliant and incisive analysis of the synthesis of biblical theology and psychology. Dr. Tan again writes with a Christlike heart, a clinical mind, and a researcher's inquisitiveness to deliver a seminal work in the field of integration. In his inimitably warm, kind, personal, humble, yet profound way, Dr. Tan leads us on a wonderful pathway of deeper understandings of God, ourselves, and others. This book is destined to become a classic for students, researchers, clinicians, and academics alike."

—JARED PINGLETON
Clinical psychologist and author of *The Struggle Is Real: How to Care for Mental and Relational Health Needs in the Church.*

"Siang-Yang Tan is about 50 percent academic scholar, 50 percent psychologist-practitioner, 50 percent pastor, and 50 percent spiritual abba and prayer warrior. And this explains why he always gives 200 percent to everything he touches. *A Christian Approach to Counseling and Psychotherapy* is no exception. . . . The modern movement concerning the integration of psychology and Christian spirituality is deeply indebted to Siang-Yang Tan. And so am I."

—GARY W. MOON
Westmont College

"Tan draws upon decades of clinical experience, pastoral care, and spiritual maturity to passionately advocate for a biblically anchored form of integration with Christ at the center. Carefully and thoughtfully guiding the reader through a detailed discussion on implicit and explicit forms of integration, then concluding with an emphasis on the Holy Spirit in clinical and counseling practice, this book is a must-read for those who want to understand the past, present, and future of Christian integration in counseling and psychotherapy."

—JOSHUA J. KNABB
California Baptist University

"I am thrilled that Tan's thoughts and wisdom, psychological and spiritual, are now available in this new volume. Tan's inclusion of and dependence on solid research as a basis for practice is an excellent source of knowledge. With the field's and society's increasing sensitivity to multicultural practice, Tan has much to offer in terms of this dimension of counseling. . . . This is an essential voice in the conversation about the relationship of our faith to psychology."

—FRED GINGRICH
Toccoa Falls College Graduate School

"No one puts it all together like Siang-Yang Tan—a widely appreciated leader in Christian counseling over the past three decades—and this accessible set of three lectures provides a helpful introduction to his thinking, practice, and contributions in Christian integration, Christian psychology, and spiritual formation."

—ERIC L. JOHNSON
Houston Baptist University

A CHRISTIAN APPROACH TO COUNSELING AND PSYCHOTHERAPY

A CHRISTIAN APPROACH TO COUNSELING AND PSYCHOTHERAPY

Christ-Centered, Biblically-Based,
and Spirit-Filled

Siang-Yang Tan

Foreword by Brad D. Strawn

 CASCADE *Books* • Eugene, Oregon

A CHRISTIAN APPROACH TO COUNSELING AND PSYCHOTHERAPY
Christ-Centered, Biblically-Based, and Spirit-Filled

Fuller School of Psychology Integration Series

Cascade Books
An Imprint of Wipf and Stock Publishers
199 W. 8th Ave., Suite 3
Eugene, OR 97401

www.wipfandstock.com

PAPERBACK ISBN: 978-1-6667-3161-3
HARDCOVER ISBN: 978-1-6667-2426-4
EBOOK ISBN: 978-1-6667-2427-1

Cataloguing-in-Publication data:

Names: Tan, Siang-Yang, author. | Strawn, Brad D., foreword.

Title: A Christian approach to counseling and psychotherapy : Christ-centered, biblically-based, and spirit-filled / by Siang-Yang Tan; foreword by Brad D. Strawn.

Description: Eugene, OR: Cascade Books, 2022 | Series: Fuller School of Psychology Integration Series | Includes bibliographical references.

Identifiers: ISBN 978-1-6667-3161-3 (paperback) | ISBN 978-1-6667-2426-4 (hardcover) | ISBN 978-1-6667-2427-1 (ebook)

Subjects: LCSH: Counseling—Religious aspects—Christianity. | Counseling. | Psychotherapy—Religious aspects—Christianity. | Psychotherapy.

Classification: BR115.C69 T36 2022 (paperback) | BR115.C69 (ebook)

VERSION NUMBER 07/18/22

This book is dedicated to all the students, faculty, and staff in the Clinical Psychology program—past, present, and future—at Fuller Theological Seminary. It is a privilege and blessing to walk the integration journey together.

CONTENTS

SERIES FOREWORD

Fuller School of Psychology Integration Series

Series editor, Brad D. Strawn, PhD
Evelyn and Frank Freed Professor for
the Integration of Psychology and Theology

The school of psychology at Fuller Theological Seminary began its unique ministry of training clinical psychologists (PhD) in Pasadena, California in 1964. The uniqueness of this training was that it was conducted in a seminary where students received an education that emphasized the integration of psychological theory and science with Christian theology. In 1972 the school of psychology was the first clinical program in a seminary to be accredited by the American Psychological Association. In 1987 it expanded its training to include the Doctor of Psychology degree, PsyD, as well as the department of marriage and family.

In those early days (and in certain quarters even today) some wondered what the two disciplines of psychology and theology could say to each other. Some thought it a contamination to integrate the two, conceiving psychology as a secular and anti-Christian science. But the pioneers at Fuller school of psychology disagreed. Rather than taking an adversarial approach, the faculty developed a variety of models for integrative dialogue, conducted empirical research in the psychology of religion, and reflected on working clinically with people of faith. Through it all Fuller has endeavored to bring the best of Christian theology (faith and practice) into honest conversation with the best of psychology (science and practice).

One of the hallmarks of the Fuller integration project is the annual Fuller Symposium on the Integration of Psychology and Theology, better known as the Integration Symposium. Each year a noted scholar working at the interface of psychology and religion is invited on campus to give a series of three lectures. These lectures include three respondents, one from the school of psychology, one from the school of theology, and one from the school of intercultural studies. In this way, the lectures and the dialogue that follows continue in this integrative dialogical tradition. Included in the *Fuller School of Psychology Integration Series* are works that have emerged from these Integration Symposium Lectures, dissertation projects that have passed with distinction, and integrative projects written by scholars both within and outside the Fuller community. The series endeavors to both preserve the rich tradition of the Integration Symposium as well as create opportunities for new dialogue in the integration of psychology and theology. This volume emerges from the lectures given by Dr. Siang-Yang Tan, professor of Clinical Psychology in February 2022.

Other volumes in the series:

Paris, Jenell. *The Good News about Conflict: Transforming Religious Struggle over Sexuality.*

Hoffman, Marie T. *When the Roll is Called: Trauma and the Soul of American Evangelicalism.*

Lee, Cameron. *Integration as Integrity: The Christian Therapist as Peacemaker.*

FOREWORD

Brad D. Strawn

The lectures published in this volume of the *Fuller Integration Lecture Series* come on the heels of Dr. Siang Yang Tan's retirement as Senior Professor of Psychology in the clinical psychology department at Fuller Theological Seminary, Pasadena, California. Before coming to Fuller, Tan earned his BA in psychology from McGill University, Montreal, Québec, Canada where he also received his PhD in clinical psychology with a dissertation on "Acute Pain in a Clinical Setting: Effects of Cognitive-Behavioural Skills Training." Dr. Tan first joined the faculty at Fuller as assistant professor in 1985 and served as Director of Practicum Training. In 1986 he became the Director of Training over Fuller's Psychological Center, which consisted of an outpatient community mental health clinic, a day-treatment program for the persistently mentally ill, and a center for aging adults. In 1989 he became the PsyD program director, was tenured in 1990, and was promoted to Professor of Psychology in 1997. During his time at Fuller, Dr. Tan has served as chair for over 57 dissertations and still counting!

Perhaps even more impressive than his lengthy service and outstanding training is what Dr. Tan has accomplished during his academic career. To say that he is a pioneer in integration would not be an overstatement! He is the author, co-author, or editor of over 22 books on topics ranging from chronic pain, lay counseling, spiritual formation, counseling, and psychotherapy from a

Christian perspective to pastoral ministry. Several of his books have been translated into Korean and Chinese. His publications in journals and contributions of book chapters take up pages in his vita. His work is sought out widely and he is featured in at least 5 professional video series. He has given countless workshops and presentations and is a widely sought out conference speaker all over the world. He has also served as an associate editor or consulting/contributing editor on some eight different professional journals.

While Dr. Tan has led a distinguished career in the broad field of psychology, it is his integrative work in psychology and theology that undoubtedly stands apart. He has served on or held leadership positions on numerous national and international boards and societies including the American Psychological Association, Division 36, Society for the Psychology of Religion and Spirituality (formerly Psychology of Religion), The American Association of Christian Counselors (AACC), and RENOVARE. He has been the recipient of numerous distinguished awards recognizing his excellence in integration including, but not limited to, the Distinguished Member Award, the highest honor from the Christian Association for Psychological Studies (CAPS), the Gary R. Collins Award for Excellence in Christian Counseling from the American Association of Christian Counselors (AACC), the William C. Bier Award for Outstanding and Sustained Contributions to the Applied Psychology of Religion from Division 36 of the American Psychological Association, and the James E. Clinton Award for Excellence in Pastoral Care and Ministry from the American Association of Christian Counselors (AACC). What all these publications, professional/academic roles, and accomplishments have in common is his love for the integration of faith and psychology and his desire that this work move from the academe to the applied setting. Dr. Tan embodies this serving as a licensed clinical practicing psychologist and an ordained and practicing Senior Pastor at First Evangelical Church in Glendale, California.

I'm one of the few fortunate persons that have known Dr. Tan as both a student and a colleague. In both settings he treated me with hospitality, respect, and encouragement. As a doctoral student I recall consulting with Dr. Tan on my dissertation because my experimental intervention utilized non-professionals functioning in therapeutic ways; so, who else would I go to but the expert on lay-counseling? After patiently and carefully listening to my design, he pointed me toward the important literature and shared his wisdom. When I joined the Fuller faculty in 2012 as the Chair of Integration, Dr. Tan was a huge supporter and encourager of my own integrative work. Dr. Tan could run circles around me related to the integration literature, but I always felt respected by him and encouraged to find my particular integrative niche. He shared books with me and read my publications, and I found him to be a life-long learner even as he prepared for the lectures in this volume.

While there are many more qualified than I to speak of his long-lasting legacy (much of that legacy can be found in these lectures) I want to end with two seminal ideas for which I believe Dr. Tan will always be remembered. Over his career there were many seminal ideas, but these continue to stand out to me, and I think will for generations to come.

First is his idea of implicit and explicit integration.[1] Speaking clinically, Dr. Tan affirmed that a well-trained clinical integrative practitioner, who had informed consent from a client, could work in religiously overt or explicit ways. The therapist might make use of scripture, prayer and spiritual resources as part of the therapy. This kind of integration is not easy to do, but it is easy to see. But Dr. Tan also spoke and wrote about implicit integration. This seminal concept may be easy to comprehend but many students and even seasoned practitioners, often lose sight of it. Dr. Tan posited that for a believing psychologist/counselor, integration could always be going on whether or not religious issues, resources or concepts appeared in the work. This implicit integration was taking place in the therapist and working its way out in the loving, caring, and healing process of therapy. This implicit integration wasn't a covert way to sneak religion into the room, but a deep recognition

1. Tan, "Religion in Clinical Practice."

that faith, religion, and spirituality would be undergirding the therapist, giving them the impetus for their work as well as the empowerment to carry it out. This radical idea suggested that a believing clinician was always doing integration!

The idea of implicit integration, working within the therapist, brings me to the second contribution for which I will always be indebted to Dr. Tan: intrapersonal integration.[2] While he wrote about the interpersonal integration that may take place in the clinical encounter, Dr. Tan always promoted the personal spirituality of the therapist—intrapersonal integration. He called his students, as he does the readers of this volume, to be Christ-centered, biblically-based and Spirit-filled. He believed it was essential that clinical integrative practitioners be engaged in their own spiritual journeys, practicing spiritual disciplines, engaging in Christian community and acts of Christian service. Again, Dr. Tan lived this out modeling it to those around him. The last year he served as regular faculty at Fuller I was able to partner with him on a student development committee. Students would be referred to our committee who were struggling in their program for a wide variety of reasons. I'll never forget how lovingly Dr. Tan opened and closed every meeting with each student in prayer and how he asked penetrating questions, deeply empathizing with each student's current challenge. He always respected their boundaries and confidence, but he could also speak a word of truth with love! It was clear to me that he was able to do all this because he himself had spent a lifetime becoming intrapersonal integrated.

I know you will be challenged, encouraged, and stimulated by the lectures in this volume. While there are many approaches to the clinical integrative endeavor, Dr. Tan's is centrally important for its unique contribution, historical context, and particular theological situatedness. I believe you will see that even in his retirement, we all continue to have much to learn from this great pioneer.

2. Tan, "Integration and Beyond," and Tan, "Intrapersonal Integration."

ACKNOWLEDGMENTS

Much of the material in these three lectures published in this book is adapted from three chapters of *Counseling and Psychotherapy: A Christian Perspective* (2nd edition) by Siang-Yang Tan published by Baker Academic, a division of Baker Publishing House (2022), and used by permission.

1

A CHRISTIAN PERSPECTIVE ON HUMAN NATURE AND EFFECTIVE COUNSELING AND PSYCHOTHERAPY

Abstract: This lecture will first briefly cover some of the latest developments in the integration of psychology and Christianity, going beyond the traditional five main views, to more embodied and relational models of integration that also specify the uniqueness and particularity of the integration task, focusing on which Christianity and which psychology are being integrated. It will also provide a biblical, Christian perspective on human nature with five basic assumptions, and on effective counseling and psychotherapy with fourteen guidelines.

I am deeply grateful and honored to be invited to be the keynote speaker for 2021's Integration Symposium, hosted by Fuller's School of Psychology & Marriage and Family Therapy. My three lectures will be on the overall theme of "A Christian Approach to Counseling and Psychotherapy: Christ-centered, Biblically-based, and Spirit-filled." My first lecture today is entitled: "A Christian Perspective on Human Nature and Effective Counseling and

Psychotherapy," based on biblical perspectives as well as the latest empirical research or evidence available. Much of the material for my three lectures is adapted from the second edition of my textbook, *Counseling and Psychotherapy: A Christian Perspective*.[1]

A BRIEF OVERVIEW OF APPROACHES TO INTEGRATION OF CHRISTIAN FAITH AND PSYCHOLOGY

I would like to begin with a brief overview, given time and space constraints, of the major approaches to integration of Christian faith and psychology. Brian Eck has summarized twenty-seven models of integration of Christian theology and psychology (including counseling and psychotherapy), using three major paradigms: the non-integrative paradigm, the manipulative paradigm, and the non-manipulative paradigm, as follows:

> The *Non-Integrative Paradigm* does not seek integration of the data but rather builds its understanding of God's truth on one discipline only. The *Manipulative Paradigm* seeks to integrate the data of both disciplines, but the data of one discipline must be altered before becoming acceptable to the other discipline. The final paradigm, the *Non-Manipulative Paradigm*, accepts the data from both disciplines directly into the integrative process.[2]

John Carter and Bruce Narramore years ago described four major approaches to integration: *Christianity against psychology* (usually held by biblically militant and more conservative Christians); *Christianity of psychology* (usually held by those with more liberal theological perspectives); the *parallels model* or *approach* (Christianity and psychology are viewed as basically separate fields but with equal importance); and *Christianity integrates psychology*.[3] Crabb has more simply labeled these four approaches

1. Tan, *Counseling and Psychotherapy.*
2. Eck, "Integrating the Integrators," 103.
3. Carter and Narramore, *Integration of Psychology and Theology.*

to integration as follows: (1) separate but equal; (2) tossed salad (equal and mixable); (3) nothing buttery (psychology is unnecessary and irrelevant because only the Bible is essential for dealing with human problems and needs); and (4) spoiling the Egyptians (using whatever concepts or techniques from secular psychology that are consistent with the Bible that has final authority).[4]

More recently, five views on the relationship of psychology and Christianity have been proposed: (1) a levels-of-explanation (scientific) view (psychology and theology are viewed as separate but equally important disciplines); (2) an integration view (psychology is taken seriously while subjecting it ultimately to Scriptural or biblical truth properly interpreted); (3) a Christian psychology view (psychology is grounded in Scripture and in biblical and historical theology); (4) a transformational psychology view (psychology is grounded in spiritual formation as psychology in the Spirit); and (5) a biblical counseling view (the Bible is used as the foundational and essential basis for counseling).[5] Similarly, five approaches to counseling and Christianity have also been described, following the five views of psychology and Christianity.[6]

Most recently, the integration field has gone beyond these five views to more personal,[7] embodied,[8] relational,[9] and community based[10] approaches. Strawn, Bland, and Flores have described three waves of integration as apologetics, model building, and empirical validation, with the more recent fourth wave of clinical integration focusing on experiential learning and clinical application, with greater diversity culturally and theologically, including

4. Crabb, *Effective Biblical Counseling.*

5. Johnson, *Psychology and Christianity.*

6. Greggo and Sisemore, *Counseling and Christianity.*

7. Sorenson, "Tenth Leper"; Sorenson et al., "National Collaborative Research on How Students Learn Integration."

8. Neff and McMinn, *Embodying Integration.*

9. Sandage and Brown, *Relational Integration of Psychology and Theology;* Sandage et al., *Relational Spirituality in Psychotherapy;* Hall and Hall, *Relational Spirituality.*

10. Strawn and Brown, *Enhancing Christian Life.*

clinical integrative practice (CIP).[11] These more recent approaches to integration go beyond abstract and more theoretical or idealistic views of integration, with an emphasis on the personal and relational experience within and between actual people, including experiential learning in a clinical context that is more culturally and theologically diverse.

Several authors have also pointed out the need to be more specific about one's particular theological tradition or perspective from which one is attempting to integrate psychology and Christianity, thus emphasizing the uniqueness and particularity of the integration task, with the key question of which Christianity and which psychology are being integrated.[12] Brad Strawn and his colleagues have pointed out that the Christianity or evangelical Christianity that is often assumed in integration with psychology is not monolithic, and a reformed theological perspective is usually used, leaving out other evangelical Christian views, such as Strawn's Wesleyan Holiness or Nazarene tradition.[13] We need to specify which Christian theology or tradition we are attempting to integrate with which particular psychology, so that we can more clearly dialogue with each other.[14]

The Wesleyan tradition is well-known for the view that there are four sources of authority: the "Wesleyan quadrilateral" consisting of Scripture, reason, tradition, and experience, with Scripture being given the highest authority.[15] However, all four sources of authority or truth need to be taken seriously in attempts at integration. For example, science and neuroscience should be seriously considered and incorporated in integration of a particular

---

11. Strawn et al., "Learning Clinical Integration"; Strawn, "Clinical Integrative Practice (CIP)."

12. Bland and Strawn, "New Conversation"; Strawn et al., "Tradition-Based Integration"; Dueck, "Babel, Esperanto, Shibboleths, and Pentecost"; Dueck and Reimer, *Peaceable Psychology*; Wright et al., "Tradition-Based Integration."

13. Strawn et al., "Tradition-Based Integration."

14. Dueck, "Babel, Esperanto, Shibboleths, and Pentecost."

15. Outler, "Wesleyan Quadrilateral in Wesley."

psychology with a particular theology.[16] Strawn and Brown recently described how extended cognition, based on a theory of mind and neuroscience, can augment religious or Christian community and enhance or "supersize" Christian life and spiritual formation that is community based and relational, and not individualistic.[17]

Neff and McMinn, in a unique daughter-father collaboration, also recently wrote about a fresh look at Christianity in the therapy room, consistent with the fourth wave of clinical integration, in what they called "embodying integration."[18] They made the following assumptions, following a postmodern perspective, in embodied integration:

1. Integration happens between people. . .Integration happens in conversation.

2. Integration is lived out in real lives, embodied in the person of the psychotherapist, which means it is more desirable to train integrators than to attempt mastering, articulating, or communicating a discipline known as "integration."

3. Integration is embedded in social and cultural contexts and therefore will have some variation to it.

4. All truth is God's truth. This is not to say that everything is true, but rather that every true thing comes from God. Christianity and psychology both belong in the conversation, and each can help transform our understanding of the other.

5. Ideas are important. Ideas explored in interaction with particular contexts are particularly meaningful.[19]

I am deeply thankful for these more recent approaches to integration that have helped us to be more humble, relational, personal, communal, and embodied in our efforts at integration. They resonate with my emphasis on personal or intrapersonal integration that includes one's spirituality, not in an individualistic sense,

16. Brown, "Resonance"; Brown and Strawn, *Physical Nature of Christian Life*.

17. Strawn and Brown, *Enhancing Christian Life*.

18. Neff and McMinn, *Embodying Integration*.

19. Neff and McMinn, *Embodying Integration*, 22.

but in a more communal or community-based context of growing together in Christ, in becoming more like Christ.[20] Integration can occur in three major areas: principled (theoretical-conceptual, and research), professional (clinical practice), and personal (or intrapersonal, including spirituality).[21] I have underscored the personal or intrapersonal area of integration, including the spirituality of the integrator, as being foundational to all integration.[22] However, I have to also honestly express my concern that we need to continue to be biblically-based and grounded in Scripture as our ultimate authority as God's inspired word (2 Tim 3:16),[23] with the best of biblical interpretation and a clear awareness of our own denominational or Christian tradition.[24] We therefore need to be humbly and prayerfully dependent on the Holy Spirit who is our teacher, par excellence, of all truth (John 14:26; 16:13), including psychotheological truth in integration, and to be in community with Christian scholars and others

My own theological perspective or Christian tradition from which I engage in integration is evangelical Christianity, with a reformed theology leaning and a charismatic orientation, or what I describe as being "biblically charismatic." I also appreciate the integration, Christian psychology, transformational psychology and biblical counseling approaches to integration. My own clinical psychology training and experience have been mainly in broad-based cognitive behavior therapy that is more relational, existential, and spiritually or biblically-based,[25] and more recently in Christian approaches to mindfulness-based cognitive behavioral

---

20. Tan, "Intrapersonal Integration"; Tan, "Integration and Beyond"; Tan, "Principled, Professional, and Personal Integration and Beyond."

21. Malony, *Integration Musings*.

22. Tan, "Intrapersonal Integration"; Tan, "Integration and Beyond."

23. Unless otherwise noted, all Scripture references are quoted from the New Revised Standard Version.

24. Porter, "Theology as Queen and Psychology as Handmaid"; Porter, "Reply to the Respondents of 'Theology as Queen and Psychology as Handmaid.'"

25. Tan, "Cognitive-Behavior Therapy"; Tan, "Use of Prayer and Scripture in Cognitive-Behavioral Therapy"; Tan, "Addressing Religion and Spirituality from a Cognitive Behavioral Perspective."

therapies.[26] I have written a few autobiographical book chapters on my life and integration journey as a Christian psychologist and pastor in a more personal, relational, embodied, and communal context that contain more details that I will briefly mention at the end of my third and final lecture.[27]

Cameron Lee, who gave the Fuller Integration Symposium lectures in 2018, has also similarly focused on the personal or intrapersonal area of integration by describing integration as a matter of personal integrity. He emphasized that the core identity of Christian therapists is as peacemakers, and the central motif of such Christ-centered integration as peacemaking, following the beatitudes of Jesus (Matt 5:3–11). As peacemakers, Christian therapists will cultivate the virtues of hope, humility, compassion, and Sabbath rest.[28]

It should be noted that while integration of Christian faith and psychology (including counseling and psychotherapy) has significantly developed in the past few decades,[29] the integration of religion and spirituality and psychotherapy in general in the secular field of counseling and psychotherapy has also considerably grown in recent years.[30] Religion and spirituality are now

---

26. Tan, "Mindfulness and Acceptance-Based Cognitive Behavioral Therapies"; Rosales and Tan, "Acceptance and Commitment Therapy (ACT)"; Rosales and Tan, "Mindfulness-Based Cognitive Therapy (MBCT)"; Wang and Tan, "Dialectical Behavior Therapy (DBT)."

27. Tan, "My Pilgrimage as a Christian Psychologist"; Tan, "Psychology Collaborating with the Church"; Tan, "My Integration Journey."

28. Lee, *Integration as Integrity*.

29. Callaway and Whitney, *Theology for Psychology and Counseling*; Hathaway and Yarhouse, *Integration of Psychology and Christianity*; Entwistle, *Integrative Approaches to Psychology and Christianity*.

30. Aten and Leach, *Spirituality and the Therapeutic Process*; Aten et al., *Spiritually Oriented Interventions for Counseling and Psychotherapy*; Cashwell and Young, *Integrating Spirituality and Religion into Counseling*; Gill and Freund, *Spirituality and Religion in Counseling*; Jones, *Spirit in Session*; Pargament, *Spiritually Integrated Psychotherapy*; Plante, *Spiritual Practices in Psychotherapy*; Richards and Bergin, *Casebook for a Spiritual Strategy for Counseling and Psychotherapy*; Richards and Bergin, *Spiritual Strategy for Counseling and Psychotherapy*; Richards and Bergin, *Handbook of Psychotherapy and Religious Diversity*; Sears and Niblick, *Perspectives on Spirituality and Religion in*

recognized, on empirical and clinical grounds, as crucial factors in psychotherapy relationships that work, and in effective counseling and psychotherapy,[31] and as a significant development in integrative therapies in general.[32]

In these lectures, I will be describing a Christian approach to counseling and psychotherapy as being Christ-centered, biblically-based, and Spirit-filled.[33] For the rest of this first lecture, I will provide five basic assumptions in a biblical perspective on human nature, and fourteen guidelines in a biblical perspective and empirically-based approach to effective counseling and psychotherapy.

A BIBLICAL PERSPECTIVE ON HUMAN NATURE

A biblical perspective on human nature or biblical anthropology is a crucial and foundational topic in integration. Much integrative and theological work has been done in recent years in this area of biblical anthropology.[34]

A biblical perspective on human nature (biblical anthropology) covers what is unique or essential in a human person,

Psychotherapy; Sperry, *Spirituality in Clinical Practice*; Sperry and Shafranske, *Spiritually Oriented Psychotherapy*; Stewart-Sicking et al., *Bringing Religion and Spirituality into Therapy*.

31. Norcross and Wampold, *Psychotherapy Relationships That Work Volume 2*; Hook et al., "Religion and Spirituality."

32. Norcross and Goldfried, *Handbook of Psychotherapy Integration 3rd Edition*.

33. Tan, *Counseling and Psychotherapy*.

34. Balswick et al., *Reciprocating Self*; Beck and Demarest, *Human Person in Theology and Psychology*; Brown et al., *Whatever Happened to the Soul?*; Corcoran, *Rethinking Human Nature*; Green, *Body, Soul, and Human Life*; Hoffman and Strawn, "Normative Thoughts, Normative Feelings, Normative Actions"; Lints et al., *Personal Identity in Theological Perspective*; Puffer, "Essential Biblical Assumptions About Human Nature"; Cortez, *Christological Anthropology in Historical Perspective*; Cortez, *Resourcing Theological Anthropology*; Crisp and Sanders, *Christian Doctrine of Humanity*; Crisp et al., *Neuroscience and the Soul*; Farris, *Introduction to Theological Anthropology*; Kilner, *Dignity and Destiny*; LaPine, *Logic of the Body*; Grudem, *Systematic Theology*.

created in the image of God (Gen 1:26–27). Christian theologians and therapists have varying views of human nature, even from a biblical perspective. In recent years, a crucial topic in biblical anthropology that has received much discussion and debate is the nature of the soul, or whether a human person even has a soul.[35] The more traditional views describe a human being as consisting of body-soul or body-mind, a form of *dualism*, or even body, soul, and spirit or *trichotomism*.[36] An alternative view that has recently gained more support is *nonreductive physicalism* that views a human person's essential nature as being synonymous with his or her physical body, including the brain, and therefore there is no separate soul of the person, with "soul" defined as the human capacity to relate to God.[37] However, the nonreductive physicalism view that attempts to incorporate neuroscience seriously in a theological context, has been strongly critiqued by other well-known Christian theologians and scholars with a more traditional or nuanced dualistic view of the human person as a body-soul being.[38]

It is still crucial to have a basic biblical perspective on human nature for guiding the process and practice of Christian counseling and psychotherapy, whether one takes a more traditional dualistic or nuanced dualistic view of the human being as a body-soul whole person or espouses a nonreductive physicalism view of human nature and the soul. Keith Puffer has provided a modest proposal of seven essential biblical assumptions about human nature,[39] summarized in the following succinct statement: "Humans are created beings fashioned into God's image. Fallen with a sinful nature and striving to find meaning, people are also redeemable, dwellable by God's Spirit, and transformable for God's

---

35. Murphy, *Nonreductive Physicalism.*

36. Murphy, *Nonreductive Physicalism*, 95–98.

37. Murphy, *Nonreductive Physicalism*; Brown, *Whatever Happened to the Soul*; Corcoran, *Rethinking Human Nature*; Green, *Body, Soul, and Human Life*; Jeeves and Brown, *Neuroscience, Psychology, and Religion.*

38. Beck and Demarest, *Human Person in Theology and Psychology*; Cooper, *Body, Soul, and Life Everlasting*; Green and Palmer, *In Search of the Soul.*

39. Puffer, "Essential Biblical Assumptions About Human Nature."

purpose."[40] He also described further implications of the following seven essential biblical assumptions about human beings as (1) created beings; (2) fashioned into God's image; (3) fallen with a sin nature; (4) striving to find meaning; (5) redeemable; (6) dwellable by the Spirit of God; (7) transformable for God's purposes.[41]

The following is a summary of a basic view of humanity or human nature from a biblical perspective that I proposed and described for effective counseling, some years ago:

1. Basic psychological and spiritual needs include needs for security (love), significance (meaning/impact), and hope (forgiveness).

2. Basic problem is sin—but not all emotional suffering is due to personal sin.

3. Ultimate goal of humanity is to know God and have spiritual health.

4. Problem feelings are usually due to problem behavior and, more fundamentally, problem thinking—however, biological and demonic factors should also be considered.

5. Holistic view of persons—all have physical, mental/emotional, social, and spiritual dimensions.[42]

This is a very basic view of human nature from a biblical perspective that is not exhaustive or even comprehensive, given the vast and complex topic of biblical anthropology. However, these five basic biblically-based assumptions of human nature have particular relevance to effective Christian counseling and psychotherapy, and will now be covered in more detail.

First, the basic psychological and spiritual needs of human beings include the needs for security (love) and significance (purpose),[43] and for hope (forgiveness).[44] The basic human needs for security and significance have also been described by Crabb as

40. Puffer, "Essential Biblical Assumptions About Human Nature," 46.

41. Puffer, "Essential Biblical Assumptions About Human Nature," 47–53.

42. Tan, *Lay Counseling*, 50–51; Tan and Scalise, *Lay Counseling*, 62–63.

43. Crabb, *Effective Biblical Counseling*.

44. Adams, *The Christian Counselor's Manual*.

"deep longings in the human heart for relationship and impact."[45] They can ultimately be met in a personal relationship with Jesus Christ as one's Lord and Savior. Such longings or needs can only be substantially satisfied in this fallen, sinful, and imperfect world, and complete fulfillment of them will only occur in heaven to come. However, they can be substantially met by surrendering our self-protective defenses and depending or leaning more fully on Jesus Christ to enable us to live our lives according to his will, by the power and presence of the Holy Spirit (Eph 5:18), including being involved in a caring community of believers, especially in a local church and small group context.

Second, from a biblical perspective, humanity's basic problem has to do with sin. All human beings have sinned and are fallen people (Rom 3:23), but we have been created in the image of God (Gen 1:26–27), with a capacity or freedom to choose (Deut 30:19; Josh 24:15). Disobedience to God's moral law as revealed in Scripture and giving in to the satanic lie or deception that we can fulfill our basic needs and longings without God are at the root of most emotional and psychological problems that do not have obvious organic bases.[46] However, this does not mean that personal sin or even the sins of others is the cause of all emotional suffering. Emotional pain can simply be an existential reality of living in a sinful, fallen, and imperfect world. Emotional anguish, even more paradoxically, can also at times have nothing to do at all with sin: it may actually be due to the process of sanctification and spiritual formation into deeper Christlikeness through the work of the Holy Spirit. Emotional pain can therefore at times be the result of obedience to God's will, and not because of sinful disobedience. Jesus himself, in the Garden of Gethsemane, experienced deep anguish and emotional and spiritual suffering as he struggled with the Father's will to die on the cross to save sinful humanity (Matt

---

45. Crabb, *Understanding People*, 45.

46. Crabb, *Effective Biblical Counseling;* see also Adams, *Christian Counselor's Manual.*

26:36–39; Mark 14:32–36; Luke 22:40–44).[47] But he never sinned (Heb 4:15).

The "dark night of the soul" as described by St. John of the Cross (Isa 50:10) is a well-known example of a mystical aspect or experience of the spiritual life in Christ that is not easily comprehended, but that is not evil or sinful but ultimately good.[48] In the words of Richard Foster:

> The 'dark night' . . . is not something bad or destructive . . .The purpose of the darkness is not to punish or afflict us. It is to set us free . . . What is involved in entering the dark night of the soul? It may be a sense of dryness, depression, even lostness. It strips us of overdependence on the emotional life . . . The dark night is one of the ways God brings us to a hush, a stillness, so that He can work on inner transformation of the soul . . . Be grateful that God is lovingly drawing you away from every distraction so that you can see Him.[49]

Christian counselors and therapists need to better understand and therefore be more sensitive, supportive, and helpful to clients who are experiencing mystical aspects of the spiritual life in Christ such as the dark night of the soul[50] or other *spiritual struggles*.[51] In this context, clients need to be helped to deal with and overcome *spiritual bypass* described as a process in which clients will use their spirituality or religious and spiritual values, beliefs, and practices as a defense to avoid painful experiences or threatening issues in their lives.[52] I have therefore previously written:

47. Grounds, *Emotional Problems and the Gospel.*

48. Coe, "Musings on the Dark Night of the Soul"; Burns, "Embracing Weakness."

49. Foster, *Celebration of Discipline,* 89–91.

50. Tan, *Intrapersonal Integration.*

51. Pargament et al., "Spiritual Struggle"; Exline, "Religious and Spiritual Struggles"; Murray-Swank and Murray-Swank, "Spiritual and Religious Problems."

52. Fox et al., "Opiate of the Masses"; Fox et al., "Religious Commitment, Spirituality, and Attitudes Toward God as Related to Psychological and Medical Help-Seeking."

From a psychological perspective, Christian psychologists need to have a better acquaintance with such processes of the spiritual life as the dark night of the soul . . . so that they do not naively or prematurely attempt to reduce all painful symptoms, but rather to appropriate their meaning first. This will require not only psychological assessment skills but spiritual wisdom and discernment as well. Sometimes there is no easy solution or therapy or healing, but to trust God and His grace to help people grow through such deepening and painful spiritual experiences. The best therapy then is to provide understanding, support, and much prayer.[53]

Third, the ultimate goal of humanity is to know God and enjoy him forever; hence spiritual health is primary. Mental and physical health are acceptable and worthwhile goals to achieve, but for the Christian they are always secondary and subordinate to the end goal of spiritual health and maturity in Christ or becoming more like Christ (Rom 8:29). This may involve suffering at times, but God has promised to give us sufficient grace and to strengthen us in our weakness (2 Cor 12:9, 10). The absence of emotional pain, or happiness at all costs, is therefore not the ultimate goal of life in this world for the Christian. Biblical perspectives on suffering[54] including "the blessings of mental anguish" as described by C. S. Evans, need to be affirmed.[55] Evans has also emphasized that "the primary goal of a Christian counselor is not to help people become merely 'normal,' but to help them love God with all their hearts, minds, and souls."[56] The ultimate goal of life and also of Christian counseling is therefore holiness in becoming more like Christ (Rom 8: 29), not temporal happiness, and spiritual health or wholeness, not just mental or physical health.[57]

53. Tan, "Intrapersonal Integration," 37.

54. Tan, "Beyond Resilience, Posttraumatic Growth, and Self-Care"; Tan, "Is Suffering Necessary for Growth?"

55. Evans, "Blessings of Mental Anguish."

56. Evans, "Blessings of Mental Anguish," 29.

57. Grounds, *Emotional Problems and the Gospel,* 105–11.

Fourth, a biblical perspective on human nature assumes that problem feelings are usually due to problem behavior (Gen 4:3–7), and more fundamentally, to problem thinking (John 8:32; Rom 12:1–2; Eph 4:22–24; Phil 4:8). Crabb has emphasized that unbiblical, erroneous basic assumptions or beliefs,[58] or what Backus has called "misbeliefs,"[59] often underlie nonorganically caused mental and emotional problems, in a basically Christian approach to cognitive therapy or rational emotive behavior therapy. However, this does not mean that problem feelings are always due to problem behavior and problem thinking. Problem feelings can also be due to biological or physical factors, even if no known organic cause can be found, given our limited but expanding knowledge of such biological factors, especially of neuroscience and brain functioning. Medical and psychiatric help should therefore be accessed where appropriate. Furthermore, problem feelings (and behaviors or thoughts) can also at times be due to demonic activity or demonization, whether demonic oppression or possession, and in such situations, after proper discernment and differential diagnosis, prayer for deliverance may be necessary, and appropriate referral to an experienced prayer ministry team in a local church may be best.[60]

Collins has emphasized the need to keep a good balance in focusing not only on problem thinking but on all three areas of human experience: feeling, behavior, and thinking.[61] Crabb has similarly described attending to the four major circles or dimensions of a person's functioning: the personal, relational, volitional, and emotional areas.[62] However, the crucial role of problem thinking and problem behavior in influencing problem feelings should still be kept in mind.

58. Crabb, *Effective Biblical Counseling*.

59. Backus, *Telling the Truth to Troubled People*; Backus and Chapian, *Telling Yourself the Truth*.

60. See Bufford, *Counseling and the Demonic*; MacNutt, *Deliverance from Evil Spirits*.

61. Collins, *How to be a People Helper*.

62. Crabb, *Understanding People*.

Fifth, and finally, a biblical perspective on human nature assumes a holistic view of persons with physical, mental-emotional, social, and spiritual dimensions (Luke 2:52), or what has also been described as a biopsychosocial-spiritual view of the whole person. Adams's total structuring approach to a client's problems in a holistic way of exploring and dealing with all areas of his or her life,[63] and Lazarus's BASIC I.D. model of one's basic identity in seven major areas of personality functioning in multimodal therapy (Behavior, Affect, Sensations, Images, Cognitions, Interpersonal relationships, Drugs/Biology) and if we add S for Spirituality, are good examples of this holistic biopsychosocial-spiritual perspective of the human person.[64]

BASIC PRINCIPLES OF EFFECTIVE COUNSELING AND PSYCHOTHERAPY: A BIBLICAL AND EVIDENCE-BASED PERSPECTIVE

I have proposed and described fourteen basic principles of effective counseling and psychotherapy from a biblical perspective that is also evidence-based. Here is a summary of the fourteen guidelines or principles for effective lay and professional counseling:

1. The Holy Spirit's ministry as counselor is crucial: depend on him (John 14:16–17; Eph 5:18).

2. The Bible is a basic and comprehensive (not exhaustive) guide for counseling (2 Tim 3:16–17).

3. Prayer is an integral part of biblical counseling (Jas 5:16).

4. The ultimate goal of counseling is maturity in Christ (Rom 8:29; 2 Pet 3:18) and fulfilling the Great Commission.

5. The personal qualities of the counselor are important, especially spiritual ones (Rom 15:14; Col 3:16; Rom 12:8; Gal 6:1–2; Gal 5:22–23).

---

63. Adams, *Christian Counselor's Manual.*
64. Lazarus, *Practice of Multimodal Therapy.*

6. The client's attitudes, motivations, and desire for help are important.

7. The relationship between counselor and client is significant.

8. Effective counseling is a process involving exploration, understanding, and action phases, with a focus on changing problem thinking.

9. The style or approach in counseling should be flexible (1 Thess 5:14).

10. Specific techniques or methods in counseling should be consistent with Scripture (1 Thess 5:21); cognitive-behavioral ones may be especially helpful, with qualifications.

11. Cultural sensitivity and cross-cultural counseling skills are required.

12. Outreach and prevention skills in the context of a caring community are important.

13. Crisis counseling is important.

14. Awareness of limitations and referral skills are also important.[65]

Due to space and time limitations for this first lecture, further elaborations and details of these fourteen guidelines or principles for effective counseling for both lay and professional counselors will not be covered here, but can be found in Tan and Tan and Scalise.[66] Empirical research for evidence-based principles and practices for effective counseling and psychotherapy in general can be found in Lambert, Norcross and Lambert, Norcross and Wampold, and Wampold and Imel, as well as Castonguay, Constantino, and Beutler, and more specifically for Christian counseling and psychotherapy in Worthington et al. and Knabb et al.[67]

---

65. Tan and Scalise, *Lay Counseling*, 62–63; Tan, *Counseling and Psychotherapy*.

66. Tan, *Counseling and Psychotherapy*; Tan and Scalise, *Lay Counseling*.

67. Lambert, *Bergin and Garfield's Handbook of Psychotherapy and Behavior Change*; Norcross and Lambert, *Psychotherapy Relationships That Work*; Norcross and Wampold, *Psychotherapy Relationships That Work*; Wampold and Imel, *Great Psychotherapy Debate*; Castonguay et al., *Principles of Change*;

For example, a well-known model based on empirical research, for looking at percent of psychotherapy outcome due to particular therapeutic factors, has the following breakdown: unexplained variance (35 percent), patient contribution (30 percent), therapy relationship (15 percent), treatment method (10 percent), individual therapist (7 percent), and other factors (3 percent).[68]

It should be noted that Tolin et al. recently made some recommendations for a new model for defining empirically supported treatments or ESTs.[69] They proposed the utilization of existing systematic reviews of all of the available outcome literature, weighting them based on the risk of bias in the outcome studies reviewed. Following grading guidelines that are generally acceptable, widely established and transparent, research findings are translated into clear recommendations of treatments as *very strong*, *strong*, or *weak*. This new model replaces the outdated original criteria used to define ESTs as *well-established efficacious treatments* and *probably efficacious treatments*. A.P.A. Division 12 (Society of Clinical Psychology) has begun using this new model to define ESTs.

In providing a biblical perspective on human nature with five basic assumptions and a biblical and evidence-based approach to effective counseling and psychotherapy with fourteen guidelines in this first lecture, as well as an overview of integration of Christian faith and psychology, I have emphasized the crucial and essential role of Christian theology in Christian counseling and psychotherapy.[70]

Worthington et al., *Evidence-Based Practices for Christian Counseling and Psychotherapy*; Knabb et al., *Christian Psychotherapy in Context*.

68. Norcross and Lambert, *Psychotherapy Relationships That Work*, 12.

69. Tolin et al., "Empirically Supported Treatment."

70. Tan, *Counseling and Psychotherapy*; see also Callaway and Whitney, *Theology for Psychology and Counseling*; Holeman, *Theology for Better Counseling*; Johnson, *Foundations for Soul Care*; Johnson, *God and Soul Care*; Lambert, *Theology of Biblical Counseling*.

2

IMPLICIT AND EXPLICIT INTEGRATION IN CHRISTIAN COUNSELING AND PSYCHOTHERAPY

Christian Faith In Clinical Practice

Abstract: This second lecture will cover implicit integration of Christian faith and counseling and psychotherapy that is a more covert approach that does not initiate the discussion of religious or spiritual issues and does not openly, directly, or systematically use spiritual resources, and explicit integration that is a more overt approach that directly and systematically deals with religious and spiritual issues in therapy, and uses spiritual resources such as prayer, Scripture or sacred texts, referrals to church or religious groups or lay counselors, and other religious practices. They are two ends of a continuum and are equally substantial and important, with the critical factor being intentional and prayerful integration, whether it involves implicit or explicit integration or both. It should be conducted in a professionally competent, ethically responsible, and clinically sensitive way, with clear informed consent from the client. Ethical guidelines will be provided for appropriately conducting integration in clinical practice. The latest empirical evidence supporting the effectiveness of religious and spiritual therapies, including Christian therapies, will also be briefly reviewed.

Christian faith in clinical practice is an example of religion or spirituality in clinical practice,[1] and refers to integration directly in the therapy room.[2] It has also been described as professional integration,[3] and the practical integration of theology and psychology.[4] It is the actual conducting of Christian counseling and psychotherapy that is Christ-centered, biblically-based, and Spirit-filled or Spirit-led.[5] This area of Christian counseling and psychotherapy, incorporating various approaches,[6] has grown tremendously, just as the more general area of religiously oriented and spiritually oriented therapy has mushroomed, in the last two decades or so, as I mentioned in my first lecture.[7] In the third wave of behavior therapy and cognitive behavior therapy, relatively contextualistic approaches that are mindfulness and acceptance-based, including acceptance and commitment therapy (ACT), mindfulness-based cognitive therapy (MBCT), and dialectical behavior therapy (DBT), have their roots in Zen Buddhism,[8] as well as other contemplative religious and spiritual traditions including Christian ones.[9] More distinctively Christian approaches to

1. Tan, "Religion in Clinical Practice."

2. Hall and Hall, "Integration in the Therapy Room"; Eck, "Exploration of the Therapeutic Use of Spiritual Disciplines in Clinical Practice."

3. Malony, *Integration Musings*; Tan, "Integration and Beyond."

4. Anderson et al., *Christ-Centered Therapy*.

5. Tan, "Integration and Beyond."

6. Worthington et al., *Evidence-Based Practices for Christian Counseling and Psychotherapy*; Bland and Strawn, *Christianity and Psychoanalysis*; Knabb et al., *Christian Psychotherapy in Context*.

7. Tan, *Counseling and Psychotherapy*.

8. Hayes, et al., "Acceptance and Commitment Therapy."

9. Tan, "Use of Prayer and Scripture in Cognitive-Behavioral Therapy"; Tan, "Mindfulness and Acceptance-Based Cognitive Behavioral Therapies"; Rosales and Tan, "Acceptance and Commitment Therapy (ACT)"; Rosales and Tan, "Mindfulness-Based Cognitive Therapy (MBCT)"; Wang and Tan,

mindfulness-based CBTs, especially ACT, have also been recently developed and described.[10] In discussing various approaches to integration of Christian faith and psychology in the first lecture, I did not mention another perspective on conducting integration directly in the therapy room, or in the clinical practice of counseling and psychotherapy. I will therefore focus on implicit and explicit integration in this second lecture as two major models on a continuum of integrating Christian faith in clinical practice.[11]

IMPLICIT AND EXPLICIT INTEGRATION IN CHRISTIAN COUNSELING AND PSYCHOTHERAPY

Christian therapy or counseling has been called consecrated counseling by Rodger Bufford who provided the following distinctives of such Christian counseling: "Counseling is truly Christian when the counselor has a deep faith; counsels with excellence; holds a Christian world view; is guided by Christian values in choosing the means, goals, and motivations of counseling; actively seeks the presence and work of God; and actively utilizes spiritual interventions and resources within ethical guidelines."[12] In this context of Christian or consecrated counseling and psychotherapy, I have described two major models of integrating Christian faith in clinical practice, as two ends of a continuum: Implicit integration and explicit integration, with the following descriptions: "*Implicit integration* . . . refers to a more covert approach that does not initiate the discussion of religious or spiritual issues and does not openly, directly or systematically use spiritual resources. . . . *Explicit integration* . . . refers to a more overt approach that directly and

"Dialectical Behavior Therapy (DBT)."

10. Knabb, *Faith-Based ACT for Christian Clients*; Knabb, *Acceptance and Commitment Therapy for Christian Clients*; Nieuwsma et al., *ACT for Clergy and Pastoral Counselors*; see also Blanton, *Contemplation and Counseling*; Coe and Strobel, *Embracing Contemplation*; Knabb, *Christian Meditation in Clinical Practice*; Trammel and Trent, *A Counselor's Guide to Christian Mindfulness*.

11. Tan, *Counseling and Psychotherapy*

12. Bufford, "Consecrated Counseling," 120.

systematically deals with spiritual or religious issues in therapy, and uses spiritual resources like prayer, Scripture and sacred texts, referrals to church or other religious groups or lay counselors, and other religious practices."[13] A Christian therapist will engage in implicit integration or explicit integration or move along the continuum between them, depending on the problems, needs, and preferences of the client, as well as the personality, inclination, and training of the Christian therapist. Both implicit integration and explicit integration are equally substantial and important. It is intentional and prayerful integration that is crucial, whether it involves implicit integration or explicit integration or both. Integration in clinical practice should be conducted in dependence on the Holy Spirit, in a professionally competent, ethically responsible, and clinically sensitive way, with clear informed consent from the client.[14] I will now provide a more detailed description of implicit integration, and then, explicit integration.

Implicit Integration in Christian Therapy

Although implicit integration is a more covert and quiet way of integrating Christian faith in clinical practice, it is also a crucial and substantial approach that is intentional and prayerfully dependent on the Holy Spirit for his help and healing presence in conducting counseling and psychotherapy with clients. The Christian therapist using implicit integration will be silently praying for the client and for the Holy Spirit to guide the therapy and touch the client in deep and healing ways, with genuine agape love, empathy, and compassion for the client. Biblical values and convictions will be quietly maintained without imposing them on the client or explicitly discussing them verbally with the client.

Implicit integration is especially helpful and appropriate when the Christian therapist is helping clients who are not believers and who are not interested at all in discussing spiritual or religious

---

13. Tan, "Religion in Clinical Practice," 368.

14. Tan, "Integration and Beyond."

issues or using any spiritual resources such as prayer or Scripture. It is also appropriate in counseling with Christian clients who are not interested in a more explicit integration approach: they may be experiencing active rebellion at God, or a significant spiritual struggle, or feeling indifferent or cold toward God, or simply prefer a more quiet, covert personal spirituality. Such clients may change over the course of therapy, and become more interested in dealing with spiritual issues more directly and even using spiritual resources more systematically, in which case the Christian therapist may move along the continuum from an implicit integration approach to a more explicit integration approach in the therapeutic process, with informed consent from the client.

Implicit integration may also be more easily and comfortably used by Christian therapists who practice from psychodynamic, psychoanalytic, or person-centered perspectives, since these therapeutic approaches are more nondirective and reflective. Explicit integration, on the other hand, may be more easily used by Christian therapists who practice from cognitive-behavioral and humanistic-existential perspectives, since these therapeutic approaches are more directive.[15]

Jeffrey Terrell has challenged my definition of implicit integration.[16] In describing an intentional incarnational approach to integration in relational psychodynamic psychotherapy, which is more normally viewed as an example of implicit integration, Terrell asserts that it can be conceptualized as "explicit" integration in another sense since it involves a very intentional use of the therapeutic relationship by the Christian therapist to facilitate deeper change in the client and his or her relational patterns: "In making this argument, I realize that I *am* blurring the boundaries of explicit and implicit integration . . . It is "explicit" in its avowal that our patient is worthy of love. It is "explicit" in its awareness of imperfection and failure in him or her. It is "explicit" in its

15. Payne et al., "Review of Attempts to Integrate Spiritual and Standard Psychotherapy Techniques."

16. Terrell, "Discussion of Intentional Incarnational Integration in Relational Psychodynamic Psychotherapy"; Tan, "Religion in Clinical Practice."

unflinching description of his or her attempts to manipulate the world. It is "explicit" in its acceptance of our patient, despite his or her worst, most humiliating experiences. In this way, intentional and incarnational integration is being practiced, whether implicit or explicit in its verbal expression."[17]

Terrell has therefore emphasized that relational psychodynamic Christian therapy that is intentional and incarnational in its approach to integration should be viewed as both "explicit" as well as implicit integration: "When we engage relationally, our patients believe we *get* them. We hear the worst and still accept them. Modeling the gospel story, our work is incarnational . . . It is redemptive, integrative, and intentional . . ., 'explicit' even when it doesn't involve the direct use of scripture texts or in session prayer."[18] Steven Rogers has also similarly described a focus on the process and the here-and-now within therapy in an object relations psychotherapy approach as a powerful and highly spiritual intervention that reflects how God interacts with human beings, and that creates a sacred space for clients to experience a deeper understanding of themselves, others, and God.[19] Bland and Strawn have more recently covered several relational psychoanalytic approaches to therapy, including attachment-based therapies, as examples of how Christian faith can be integrated in psychoanalytic therapy, in their edited book focusing on a new integrative conversation between Christianity and psychoanalysis.[20]

Explicit Integration in Christian Therapy

Explicit integration is a more overt approach to integrating Christian faith into clinical practice. The Christian therapist who engages in explicit integration in Christian counseling and psychotherapy

17. Terrell, "Discussion of Intentional Incarnational Integration in Relational Psychodynamic Psychotherapy," 162.

18. Terrell, "Discussion of Intentional Incarnational Integration in Relational Psychodynamic Psychotherapy," 164.

19. Rogers, "Where the Moment Meets the Transcendent."

20. Bland and Strawn, *Christianity and Psychoanalysis.*

will more verbally, directly, and systematically deal with spiritual and religious issues in therapy and use spiritual resources such as prayer, Scripture, referrals to church or other support groups or lay counselors, and other religious practices or spiritual disciplines. In explicit integration, psychological therapy is also being integrated with spiritual guidance or spiritual direction to some extent, in the context of therapy.[21]

Explicit integration in Christian therapy should be conducted in a clinically sensitive, ethically responsible, and professionally competent way. It can be potentially misused by over enthusiastic therapists or insensitive therapists who may unethically impose their spiritual interventions and religious values on clients, especially without obtaining informed consent first from clients.[22] Several ethical guidelines need to be followed in the appropriate and ethical practice of explicit integration in Christian therapy.[23] They include the following three basic practices proposed by Nelson and Wilson for the ethical use of religious faith in therapy by Christian therapists, if: (1) they are dealing with clinical problems that can benefit from religious or spiritual interventions; (2) they are not imposing their own religion's beliefs and values on the client and are thus working within the client's belief system; and (3) they have obtained informed consent from the client to use religious or spiritual resources and interventions as part of a clearly defined therapy contract with the client.[24]

It is crucial for a Christian therapist to sensitively and openly discuss with the client in the initial intake interview or first session, how the client would like to deal with spiritual and religious issues, if at all, in deciding whether to take an implicit or explicit integration approach in therapy. Helpful questions the therapist

21. Tan, "Religion in Clinical Practice"; Tan, "Integrating Spiritual Direction into Psychotherapy."

22. Tan, "Religion in Clinical Practice."

23. Tan, "Integrating Spiritual Direction into Psychotherapy"; Chapelle, "A Series of Progressive Legal and Ethical Decision-Making Steps for using Christian Spiritual Interventions in Psychotherapy"; Hathaway, "Clinical Use of Explicit Religious Approaches"; Sanders, *Christian Counseling Ethics*.

24. Nelson and Wilson, "Ethics of Sharing Religious Faith in Psychotherapy."

can ask the client in the intake interview include: "What is your religion or religious affiliation, if any?" and "Are religious or spiritual issues and resource such as prayer important for you and me to address in our therapy sessions?" If the client is not interested in dealing with religious or spiritual issues or using spiritual resources in therapy, then the therapist needs to respect the client's wishes and not engage in explicit integration but use implicit integration instead. If the client is interested in a more explicit integration approach, the therapist can then proceed to obtain informed consent from the client, preferably in written form, so that the therapy contract with the client clearly includes open discussion of religious or spiritual issues and the use of spiritual resources such as prayer and Scripture in therapy. It will also include the goals for therapy as set by the client. However, if the therapist does not feel adequately trained or experienced in using an explicit integration approach in therapy, then the therapist should refer the client to another Christian therapist who may be more experienced in conducting explicit integration in Christian therapy.[25]

Implicit and explicit integration are not two mutually exclusive models for integrating Christian faith in therapy or clinical practice. They are to be viewed as two ends of a continuum. A Christian therapist's integration approach can range from being implicit to explicit, and also include moving along the continuum with the client, at different stages of the therapy, and even during a particular therapy session, depending on the needs and interest or openness of the client. The therapist needs to respond to the client in an appropriate, empathic, and sensitive way. As Terrell has emphasized, a more relational psychodynamic approach to therapy, while relatively more implicit, can also be considered to be "explicit" in its intentional and incarnational integration, even if it is not always direct or verbal in dealing with religious issues.[26]

Explicit integration in Christian therapy has various components. Three major aspects of explicit integration that I will now

25. Tan, "Religion in Clinical Practice."

26. Terrell, "Discussion of Intentional Incarnational Integration in Relational Psychodynamic Psychotherapy."

cover in more detail are: (1) using religious and spiritual resources in therapy; (2) dealing with spiritual issues in therapy; and (3) fostering intrapersonal integration and the development of spirituality in both the therapist and client.[27]

Explicit Integration: Use of Religious and Spiritual Resources in Therapy

The open, direct, and systematic use of religious and spiritual resources in therapy is a major component of explicit integration. There are many different examples of such resources in spiritually oriented or religiously accommodative therapies in general.[28] The three major ones I will cover in this lecture are: prayer, Scripture, and referral to religious groups more specifically in explicit integration in Christian counseling and psychotherapy.[29]

PRAYER

Prayer is a major spiritual resource or intervention that is often used in explicit integration. It can be simply described as

27. Tan, "Religion in Clinical Practice."

28. Aten and Leach, *Spirituality and the Therapeutic Process*; Aten et al., *Spiritually Oriented Interventions for Counseling and Psychotherapy*; Cashwell and Young, *Integrating Spirituality and Religion into Counseling*; Gill and Freund, *Spirituality and Religion in Counseling*; Jones, *Spirit in Session*; Pargament, *Spiritually Integrated Psychotherapy*; Pargament et al., *APA Handbook of Psychology, Religion, and Spirituality*; Plante, *Spiritual Practices in Psychotherapy*; Richards and Bergin, *Handbook of Psychotherapy and Religious Diversity*; Sears and Niblick, *Perspectives on Spirituality and Religion in Psychotherapy*; Sperry, *Spirituality in Clinical Practice*; Sperry and Shafranske, *Spiritually Oriented Psychotherapy*; Walker et al., *Spiritually Oriented Therapy for Trauma*; Walker and Hathaway, *Spiritual Interventions in Child and Adolescent Psychotherapy*.

29. Tan, "Religion in Clinical Practice"; Appleby and Ohlschlager, *Transformative Encounters*; Knabb et al., *Christian Psychotherapy in Context*; Sbanotto et al., *Skills for Effective Counseling*; Thomas, *Counseling Techniques*; Thomas and Sosin, *Therapeutic Expedition*; Worthington et al., *Evidence-Based Practices for Christian Counseling and Psychotherapy*.

communing with God, but it also includes other ways of experiencing or focusing on God.[30] The following are some examples or types of prayer: *meditative* (waiting and worshiping in God's presence), *ritualistic* (involving the use of rituals), *petitionary* (making specific requests), and *colloquial* (conversational and relational, with gratitude) prayer,[31] as well as *intercessory* (asking on behalf of others, e.g., for their healing and blessing) prayer.[32] A specific form of prayer is called "holy name repetition," and Christian examples include "Lord, Jesus Christ, Son of God, have mercy on me," "Lord Jesus have mercy," or just "Jesus," all variants of the well-known Jesus prayer that is often used to "pray continually" (1 Thess 5:17),[33] especially in the Eastern Orthodox Church tradition.[34] Richard Foster has described twenty-one types of prayer for *moving inward* to seek the transformation we need, *moving upward* to seek the intimacy we need, and *moving outward* to seek the ministry we need.[35] More simply, many Christians have learned the major types of prayer by using the acrostic ACTS for Adoration, Confession, Thanksgiving, and Supplication (including both petition for oneself and intercession for others).

Different types of prayer can therefore be used in Christian therapy with a client, such as quiet, meditative, or contemplative prayer, general prayer aloud with the client, specific prayer aloud with and for the client, and inner healing prayer or prayer for healing of memories. A Christian therapist can also use prayer in explicit integration at different times as appropriate and sensitive to the needs of the client and the leading of the Holy Spirit: before, during, or after the therapy session, at the beginning or at the end

---

30. Johnson, "Religious Resources in Psychotherapy."

31. Poloma and Pendleton, "Exploring Types of Prayer and Quality of Life"; Poloma and Pendelton, "Effects of Prayer and Prayer Experiences on Measures of General Well-Being."

32. McCullough and Larson, "Prayer."

33. Oman and Driskill, "Holy Name Repetition as a Spiritual Exercise and Therapeutic Technique."

34. Vasquez and Jensen, "Practicing the Jesus Prayer."

35. Foster, *Prayer.*

of the therapy session, or at any other time connected with the therapy session.

Christian contemplative prayer focuses on giving one's full attention on relating to God in an open, passive, nondefensive, and nondemanding way, and can be used in explicit integration.[36] However, such contemplative prayer, or any other type of prayer, should not be used simply as a therapeutic technique or coping strategy for more effective anxiety management,[37] but appropriately used only if spiritual growth is also a goal of therapy. Prayer should therefore not just be a tool, technique, or strategy in therapy, but it should be viewed as an end in itself.[38] Prayer should be a way of life for the Christian in relationship with God.[39] Prayer can be described as "the transforming friendship"[40] with God in which we find our heart's true home in loving, intimate relationship with God.[41] Relational prayer should therefore come before petitionary prayer.[42] Prayer has also been described as a "tree of life" that unifies Christian spirituality, with five major models of prayer: conversation, relationship, journey, transformation, and presence.[43] Two major traditions of prayer have been historically labelled as *apophatic* or mainly wordless prayer, and *kataphatic* or mainly prayer with words.[44]

Joshua Knabb and Thomas Frederick have recently developed an eight-week Christian contemplative prayer program to

---

36. Finney and Malony, "Empirical Study of Contemplative Prayer as an Adjunct to Psychotherapy"; Finney and Malony, "Contemplative Prayer and its Use in Psychotherapy"; Finney and Malony, "Empirical Studies of Christian Prayer."

37. Finney and Malony, "Contemplative Prayer and its Use in Psychotherapy."

38. Hunsinger, *Pray Without Ceasing*.

39. Johnson, "Religious Resources in Psychotherapy."

40. Houston, *Transforming Friendship*.

41. Foster, *Prayer*.

42. Crabb, *PAPA Prayer*; Strobel and Coe, *Where Prayer Becomes Real*.

43. Chase, *Tree of Life*.

44. Egan, "Christian Apophatic and Kataphatic Mysticisms"; Knabb and Frederick, *Contemplative Prayer for Christians with Chronic Worry*, 24–25.

help Christians struggling with chronic worry.[45] It richly draws from Scripture as well as the practices of the early desert Christians and others throughout church history, with an emphasis on contemplative prayer for overcoming chronic worry and anxiety. It includes helpful daily exercises (for at least 20 minutes) and the following examples of contemplative prayer: the serenity prayer, Ignatian contemplation, the Jesus prayer, centering prayer, and the welcoming prayer.[46] This God-centered Christian meditation and contemplative prayer approach has received some preliminary empirical support for its effectiveness with repetitive negative thinking,[47] recurrent worry,[48] daily stress,[49] and with shifting from trauma-based ruminations to ruminating on God.[50]

Inner healing prayer or *healing of memories* is a specific type of prayer that has been defined as "a form of prayer designed to facilitate the client's ability to process affectively painful memories through vividly recalling those memories and asking for the presence of Christ (or God) to minister in the midst of this pain."[51] Fernando Garzon and Lori Burkett reviewed four major models of healing of memories developed by David Seamands, myself, Leanne Payne, and Edward Smith who is the founder of Theophostic Ministry, and pointed out their similarities and differences.[52] They also traced the history of healing of memories back to Agnes Sanford in the 1950s, and the subsequent work of others such as Francis

---

45. Knabb and Frederick, *Contemplative Prayer for Christians with Chronic Worry.*

46. See also Knabb, *Christian Meditation in Clinical Practice.*

47. Knabb et al., "Christian Meditation for Repetitive Negative Thinking"; Knabb et al., "'Unknowing' in the 21st Century."

48. Knabb et al., "Surrendering to God's Providence."

49. Knabb and Vasquez, "Randomized Controlled Trial of a 2-Week Internet-Based Contemplative Prayer Program for Christians with Daily Stress."

50. Knabb et al., "Set Your Minds on Things Above."

51. Garzon and Burkett, "Healing of Memories," 42.

52. Garzon and Burkett, "Healing of Memories"; Seamands, *Healing of Memories*; Tan, "Religion in Clinical Practice"; Payne, *Restoring the Christian Soul*; Smith, *Healing Life's Hurts Through Theophostic Prayer.*

MacNutt, Ruth Carter Stapleton, and John and Paula Sandford.[53] Inner healing prayer can be especially helpful to clients with unresolved painful memories from their past having to do with experiences such as deprivation or neglect, rejection, abandonment, harsh treatment or criticism, physical or sexual abuse, and trauma. It can therefore be a useful spiritual resource or intervention in explicit integration in Christian therapy. It has recently been described as part of a Christian multi-modal approach to therapy called "the Life Model."[54] Inner healing prayer should be used in a clinically sensitive way, always with the informed consent of the client. Garzon and Burkett have suggested that it should not be used, or used only with caution, with clients who have substance abuse problems, thought disorders, severe depression, or burnout.[55] In such cases, the therapist should engage in adequate assessment of the client, proper timing, and comprehensive treatment.

I have developed a seven-step model for inner healing prayer that was first described in 1992.[56] There is no set script for the client or specific images of Jesus to be visualized, unlike some other approaches to healing of memories.[57] The focus in my model is on prayer and the Holy Spirit's presence and ministry during the inner healing prayer process, with the emphasis on waiting upon the Lord to minister to the client in whatever way the Spirit leads. The seven steps for inner healing prayer are as follows:

1. "Begin with prayer for protection from evil, and ask for the power and healing ministry of the Holy Spirit to take control of the session.

53. See also Flynn and Gregg, *Inner Healing*; Kraft, *Deep Wounds, Deep Healing*; Lee, *The Importance of Inner Healing and Deliverance for Effective Discipleship*; Richardson, *Experiencing Healing Prayer*; Wardle, *Healing Care, Healing Prayer*.

54. Wilder et al., "Christian Multi-Modal Approach to Therapy Utilizing Inner-Healing Prayer."

55. Garzon and Burkett, "Healing of Memories."

56. Tan, "Holy Spirit and Counseling Ministries"; Tan, "Religion in Clinical Practice"; Tan, "Inner Healing Prayer"; Tan and Ortberg, *Coping with Depression*, 64–71.

57. Seamands, *Healing of Memories*.

2. Guide the client into a relaxed state, usually by brief relaxation strategies (e.g., slow, deep breathing, calming self-talk, pleasant imagery, prayer, and Bible imagery).

3. Guide the client to focus attention on a painful past event or traumatic experience, and to feel deeply the pain, hurt, anger, and so forth.

4. Prayerfully ask the Lord, by the power of the Holy Spirit, to come to the client and minister his comfort, love, and healing grace (even gentle rebuke where necessary). It may be Jesus imagery, or other healing imagery, music (song/hymn), Scripture, a sense of his presence or warmth, or other manifestation of the Spirit's working. No specific guided imagery or visualization is provided or directively given at this point.

5. Wait quietly upon the Lord to minister to the client with his healing grace and truth. Guide and speak only if necessary and led by the Holy Spirit. In order to follow or track with the client, the counselor will periodically and gently ask, "What's happening? What are you feeling or experiencing now?"

6. Close in prayer.

7. Debrief and discuss the inner healing prayer experience with the client."[58]

If appropriate and the client is open to doing so, homework inner healing prayer can be assigned to the client to be incorporated into his or her own times of prayer at home. This seven-step model for inner healing prayer can be adapted or modified where necessary.[59]

Inner healing prayer may not proceed smoothly along these seven steps for some clients, especially those who may not be able to recall or relive their painful memories in imagery, in which case, they can simply tell their painful stories verbally in a narrative approach and pray over them. Another option is for the therapist to role-play the painful situation with the client and then end with prayer. Clients may need reassurance that the Lord will give them sufficient grace even if they do not experience significant healing

---

58. Tan, *Inner Healing Prayer*, 20–21.

59. Tan, "Use of Prayer and Scripture in Cognitive-Behavioral Therapy."

after inner healing prayer (see 2 Cor 12:9–10). The importance and necessity of forgiveness in the process of inner healing should also be emphasized and addressed.

There is a need for better-controlled outcome research on the effectiveness of inner healing prayer for the healing of past painful memories or experiences, and not simply prayer with Jesus imagery for dealing with present and future-oriented situations,[60] as Garzon and Burkett have pointed out.[61]

Another type of prayer that needs to be briefly mentioned is prayer for deliverance from evil spirits or sometimes called exorcism. Prayer for deliverance may be needed if a client shows signs of being demonized or oppressed by demons or evil spirits.[62] Many Christian therapists may prefer to refer such clients to a deliverance specialist or pastors, pastoral counselors, or prayer ministry teams in local churches who may have more experience or training in deliverance ministries, because this is a controversial area that may have legal risks.[63] If there is a need to deal with a client who is clearly experiencing demonization, and with informed consent, the Christian therapist can pray for deliverance as follows: "In the name of Jesus, I command you to leave this person now, and go where Jesus sends you, never to return again to oppress or afflict this person."

Prayer can of course be potentially misused or abused in therapy, and there are some dangers in the superficial use of inner healing interventions,[64] such as using prayer to escape from dealing with deeper and more painful issues in therapy, a process

---

60. Propst et al., "Comparative Efficacy of Religious and Nonreligious Cognitive-Behavioral Therapy for the Treatment of Clinical Depression in Religious Individuals."

61. Garzon and Burkett, "Healing of Memories."

62. Appleby, *It's Only a Demon*; Appleby, "Deliverance as Part of the Therapeutic Process"; Bufford, *Counseling and the Demonic*; MacNutt, *Deliverance from Evil Spirits*; Lee, *Importance of Inner Healing and Deliverance for Effective Discipleship*.

63. Appleby, *Deliverance as Part of the Therapeutic Process*.

64. Alsdurf and Malony, "Critique of Ruth Carter Stapleton's Ministry of 'Inner Healing'"; Malony, "Inner Healing."

that has been more recently described as spiritual bypass.[65] Some Christian therapists have therefore urged caution but not censure in explicit integration involving the use of prayer and Scripture in therapy sessions.[66] However, prayer and inner healing prayer can be used in a helpful and effective way with highly spiritual or religious clients such as orthodox or conservative Christians, who may prefer the explicit use of prayer and Scripture and open discussion of religious and spiritual issues and concerns.[67] Prayer should not be imposed on Christian clients, because some of them may not be interested in incorporating prayer into their therapy, especially those who are more liberal, Catholic, and younger, but the majority (82 percent) of first-visit Christian clients have been found to want audible prayer in counseling in one survey.[68]

A client's level of religious commitment should also be assessed before proceeding with the use of spiritual resources such as prayer in therapy sessions. Clients with high religious commitment have been found to have greater improvement in their presenting problem after receiving religiously tailored interventions explicitly in Christian therapy compared to those with low religious commitment.[69]

A study on prayer and subjective well-being found that of six prayer types (adoration, confession, thanksgiving, supplication, reception, and obligatory prayer), three (adoration, thanksgiving, and reception with a contemplative attitude of openness, receptivity, and surrender) were positively related to well-being,[70] and they were more God-focused than ego-focused. In another study on the functions of prayer in the coping process, the most effective were

65. Fox et al., "Opiate of the Masses."

66. McMinn, *Psychology, Theology, and Spirituality in Christian Counseling*; McMinn and McRay, "Spiritual Disciplines and the Practice of Integration."

67. Gass, "Orthodox Christian Values Related to Psychotherapy and Mental Health"; Rose et al., "Spiritual Issues in Counseling."

68. Weld and Eriksen, "Christian Clients' Preferences Regarding Prayer as a Counseling Intervention."

69. Wade et al., "Effectiveness of Religiously Tailored Interventions in Christian Therapy."

70. Whittington and Scher, "Prayer and Subjective Well-Being."

the prayer functions of seeking guidance and expressing gratitude according to participants' reports.[71]

Prayer has also been categorized as inward prayer (focusing on oneself), outward prayer (focusing on others), and upward prayer (focusing on the divine or higher power) by Ladd and Spilka.[72] Some recent research has shown that inward, outward, and upward prayer are associated with internal dialogue, but only upward prayer mediated the relationship between internal dialogue and well-being.[73] In another study, those in the inward prayer and outward prayer conditions felt more resolved, at peace, and content than participants in the thought condition. They also had significantly greater cognitive understanding of a personal problem.[74] Spilka and Ladd have written a comprehensive treatment of the psychology of prayer from a scientific approach.[75]

SCRIPTURE

The use of Scripture or the Bible (and other sacred texts in other religious approaches to therapy) is a second major example of the use of religious and spiritual resources in explicit integration in Christian therapy, especially in Christian CBT.[76] The Bible as God's inspired word (2 Tim 3:16) can be used in helpful ways in Christian therapy, for different purposes including "to comfort, clarify (guide), correct (cognitively restructure), change character, cleanse, convict (convert), and cure (heal) (e.g., see 2 Tim. 3:16;

71. Bade and Cook, "Functions of Christian Prayer in the Coping Process."

72. Ladd and Spilka, "Inward, Outward, Upward"; Ladd and Spilka, "Inward, Outward, Upward Prayer."

73. Puchalska-Wasyl and Zarzycka, "Prayer and Internal Dialogical Activity."

74. Parks-Stamm et al., "Impact of Prayer Direction on Emotional and Cognitive Responses to Personal Problems."

75. Spilka and Ladd, *Psychology of Prayer.*

76. Tan, "Use of Prayer and Scripture in Cognitive-Behavioral Therapy"; Tan, "Addressing Religion and Spirituality from a Cognitive Behavioral Perspective"; Tan and Johnson, "Spiritually Oriented Cognitive-Behavioral Therapy."

John 15:3; Ps. 119:9, 11; Heb. 4:12; 1 Pet. 2:2; Ps. 119:105; Ps. 119:97–100; 1 Pet. 1:23; Rom. 10:17; John 8:32)."[77]

Scripture can be used in Christian therapy in different ways such as: indirectly by alluding to biblical truth; directly but generally by referring to teachings or examples in the Bible without citing chapter and verse; directly and specifically by referring to particular texts of Scripture, citing chapter and verse; by reading, meditating, memorizing, hearing, or studying Scripture;[78] or by assigning Scripture for homework reading, study, meditation, or memorization.[79]

Fernando Garzon has described several therapeutic interventions that apply Scripture in therapy,[80] as well as a Christian devotional meditation approach for anxiety using Scriptural truth meditation that is God-centered, focusing either on God's character or on a specific Bible text.[81] Mindfulness-based interventions have also been adapted for conservative Christians, by using more God-centered Christian accommodative breath meditation and Christian-accommodative loving kindness meditation.[82] Meditation, prayer, and contemplation based on Scripture as Christian practices in counseling and psychotherapy (e.g., Ignatian spirituality, medieval apophatic contemplation, Puritan practices of meditation and contemplation, Immanuel Prayer Approach and inner healing prayer in the Life Model, and the Jesus Prayer) are receiving more attention in both research and clinical application.[83]

---

77. Tan, "Use of Prayer and Scripture in Cognitive-Behavioral Therapy," 108.

78. Tan and Gregg, *Disciplines of the Holy Spirit*, 79–91.

79. Tan, "Use of Prayer and Scripture in Cognitive-Behavioral Therapy," 108.

80. Garzon, "Interventions that Apply Scripture in Psychotherapy."

81. Garzon, "Christian Devotional Meditation for Anxiety."

82. Garzon and Ford, "Adapting Mindfulness for Conservative Christians"; Blanton, *Contemplation and Counseling*; Coe and Strobel, *Embracing Contemplation*.

83. Knabb et al., "Introduction to the Special Issue." See also Ford and Garzon, "Research Note"; Jones et al., "Christian Accomodative Mindfulness"; Trammel, "Effectiveness of an MP3 Christian Mindfulness Intervention";

The use of Scripture in Christian therapy is especially relevant and useful in Christian cognitive behavior therapy or CBT with a focus on cognitive restructuring of dysfunctional thinking that may include unbiblical or sinful assumptions and misbeliefs. Standard questions used in secular CBT for cognitive restructuring include the following: "On what basis do you say this? Where is the evidence for your conclusion?", "Is there another way of looking at this?", and "If your conclusion is true, what does it mean to you?" In Christian CBT, Scripture is often used to challenge unbiblical and distorted thinking, using questions such as: "What do you think the Bible has to say about this?" or "What do you think God has to say about this?"[84] There are several helpful resources that a Christian therapist can use as quick Scripture references for counseling, but careful biblical interpretation is needed in using any biblical texts.[85]

Scripture can also be potentially abused or misused in Christian therapy.[86] In order to avoid using Scripture in a superficial or insensitive way that can be potentially harmful to a client, Monroe has suggested that Christian therapists ask themselves the following questions to clarify why they may want to use Scripture in therapy sessions with their clients: "Why do I want to have them read this text? What do I hope to accomplish through it (e.g., to be provoked, taught, comforted, connected to something greater than self, to change one's focal point, etc.)? What barriers might hinder this goal? How might they misinterpret my intervention?"[87]

Trammel et al., "Religiously Oriented Mindfulness for Social Workers."

84. Tan, "Use of Prayer and Scripture in Cognitive-Behavioral Therapy," 108; Tan, "Addressing Religion and Spirituality from a Cognitive Behavioral Perspective."

85. Kruis, *Quick Scripture Reference for Counseling*; Miller, *Quick Scripture Reference for Counseling Men*; Miller and Miller, *Quick Scripture Reference for Counseling Youth*; Miller, *Quick Scripture Reference for Counseling Women*; Crabb, *66 Love Letters*.

86. Johnson, "Religious Resources in Psychotherapy."

87. Monroe, "Guidelines for the Effective Use of the Bible in Counseling," 56.

Referrals to Religious Groups

Referrals to religious groups such as churches or parachurch groups that are within the client's religious belief system is a third major example of the use of religious and spiritual resources in explicit integration in Christian therapy. These religious groups often provide support, fellowship, and prayer that can be helpful for the client's healing and growth. They can also contribute to the client's making a better transition through the termination phase of therapy. Such religious groups include: "small groups, Bible study groups, recovery groups, prayer groups, fellowship groups, religiously oriented or Christ-centered 12-step programs, youth groups, and so forth."[88]

Lay counseling services are also often available without charge in churches and parachurch organizations, to which clients can be referred for further support and help, especially if they cannot afford to have or continue professional therapy. The lay or paraprofessional counselors in churches and parachurch groups are often carefully selected, trained, and supervised in a systematic way, and can provide helpful and effective services.[89]

Referral to religious groups can be of benefit to clients open to such ministries or services, but it should be done in a supportive and sensitive way, in full collaboration with the client.

Explicit Integration: Dealing with Spiritual Issues in Therapy

A second major component of explicit integration is dealing with spiritual issues in therapy. Clients often seek help from counselors and psychotherapists because of problems that have spiritual or moral aspects and even roots or causes.[90] Explicit integration in clinical practice will involve dealing with such religious and

88. Tan, "Religion in Clinical Practice," 376.

89. Tan and Scalise, *Lay Counseling*; Tan, *Shepherding God's People*.

90. Crabb, *Understanding People*; White, "Spiritual and Religious Issues in Therapy."

spiritual issues presented by the client directly and openly with the client, with full informed consent given by the client. The first step is to conduct an initial and adequate spiritual assessment of the client and the problems being presented. Kenneth Pargament has suggested the following helpful questions to use in an initial spiritual assessment of the client in an intake interview: "'Do you see yourself as a religious or spiritual person? If so, in what way?' (assessing the salience of spirituality to the client); 'Are you affiliated with a religious or spiritual denomination or community? If so, which one' (assessing the salience of a religious affiliation to the client); 'Has your problem affected you religiously or spiritually? If so, in what way?' (assessing the salience of spirituality to the problem); and, 'Has your religion or spirituality been involved in the way you have coped with your problem? If so, in what way?' (assessing the salience of spirituality to the solution)."[91]

Other suggestions for conducting an initial religious or spiritual assessment of the client can be found in H. N. Malony's religious status interview and M. Scott Peck's questions for taking a spiritual history.[92]

Spiritual and religious issues can also emerge later in therapy with clients. They can include broader existential struggles such as searching for meaning in life, dealing with the fear of death and mortality, and choosing authentic values in life.[93] They can also include more specific spiritual and religious issues such as doubts, sins, struggles with guilt, bitterness, and unforgiveness, "dark nights of the soul" and other spiritual struggles,[94] and even possible demonization. Negative aspects of spiritual and religious experiences such as toxic faith or religious addiction may also need to be explicitly addressed in therapy.[95]

91. Pargament, *Spiritually Integrated Psychotherapy*, 211.

92. Malony, "Clinical Assessment of Optimal Religious Functioning"; Peck, *Further Along the Road Less Traveled*.

93. Wong et al., *Positive Psychology of Meaning and Spirituality*.

94. Pargament, *Spiritually Integrated Psychotherapy*.

95. Arterburn and Felton, *Toxic Faith*; Booth, *When God Becomes a Drug*.

Gary Collins has described the following list of several spiritual issues that may often be encountered in Christian therapy: "sinful thoughts and actions; legalism; self-sufficiency; pride; bitterness; non-Christian values; lack of: understanding of spiritual issues, spiritual nourishment, giving, balance, commitment, simplicity, Holy Spirit power, spiritual disciplines, and involvement with the church; suffering; and spiritual warfare."[96]

The Christian therapist needs to explore and address spiritual and religious issues with the client in an empathic and supportive way, with gentleness, deep respect, and compassion for the client, without imposing the therapist's own religious convictions or beliefs on the client. Timing is crucial in this context, especially in dealing with spiritual struggles and conflicts. The client's faith can be negatively affected if these difficult and painful issues are confronted too soon or insensitively. Following the client's lead and pacing the therapy in an empathic way will be necessary, always respecting the client's freedom to choose and make ultimate decisions. For more severely disturbed clients, the therapist will wisely refrain from confronting or challenging their religious beliefs, even if they are obviously dysfunctional or detrimental, until the clients have emotionally stabilized and are more ready to deal with their religious misbeliefs.[97]

It is also crucial for Christian therapists to learn how to sensitively help clients from different and diverse religions and cultural backgrounds by having some understanding of other religions.[98] Robert Lovinger has provided some helpful examples of countertransference on the part of the therapist in dealing explicitly with religious issues in therapy with religiously committed clients, that therapists need to be careful not to fall into, such as: arguing with clients about doctrinal issues; having long discussions about philosophical and theological topics with no therapeutic purpose; and not adequately exploring the reasons for a sudden or significant

---

96. Collins, *Christian Counseling*, 825.

97. Tan, "Religion in Clinical Practice."

98. Richards and Bergin, *Handbook of Psychotherapy and Religious Diversity*.

change in religious orientation in the client, especially in the direction of the therapist's own denomination or religion.[99]

Explicit Integration: Fostering Intrapersonal Integration and the Development of Spirituality in the Therapist and the Client

A third major component of explicit integration in Christian therapy is fostering intrapersonal or personal integration (i.e., one's own appropriation of faith and integration of psychological and spiritual experience) and the spiritual development of the therapist and client.[100] Explicit integration often includes the discussion and application of spiritual disciplines as means of God's grace for spiritual formation or growing into deeper Christlikeness (Rom 8:29) and spiritual maturity (2 Pet 3:18). There are now many books available that clearly describe the traditional spiritual disciplines as ancient practices for Christian spiritual growth and transformation.[101] For example, in *Disciplines of the Holy Spirit*, Tan and Gregg describe the following spiritual disciplines: disciplines of solitude in drawing near to God (solitude and silence, listening and guidance, prayer and intercession, and study and meditation); disciplines of surrender in yielding to God (repentance and confession, yielding and submission, fasting, and worship); disciplines of service in reaching out to others (fellowship, simplicity, service, and witness).[102] Adele Calhoun recently listed

---

99. Lovinger, *Working with Religious Issues in Therapy.*

100. Tan, "Religion in Clinical Practice."

101. Foster, *Celebration of Discipline*; Tan and Gregg, *Disciplines of the Holy Spirit*; Whitney, *Spiritual Disciplines for the Christian Life*; Willard, *The Spirit of the Disciplines*; Bennet, *Practices of Love*; Calhoun, *Spiritual Disciplines Handbook*; Comer, *Ruthless Elimination of Hurry*; Ortberg, *Life You've Always Wanted*; Ortberg, *Soulkeeping*; Shigematsu, *Survival Guide for the Soul*; Warren, *Liturgy of the Ordinary*.

102. Tan and Gregg, *Disciplines of the Holy Spirit.*

and described seventy-five spiritual disciplines as practices that can transform us.[103]

Spiritual disciplines, however, can be potentially dangerous,[104] especially if they are practiced in a legalistic and self-absorbed way that can lead to pride, self-sufficiency, and self-righteousness, with ultimate harm to one's spiritual life and development. It is crucial therefore to also focus on what Gary Thomas has called the *authentic disciplines* or *circumstantial spiritual disciplines* that are not in our voluntary control, but initiated or allowed by God, as vital additions to the traditional spiritual disciplines.[105] The authentic disciplines include selflessness, waiting, suffering, persecution, social mercy, forgiveness, mourning, contentment, sacrifice, and hope and fear.[106] They focus more on God seeking the face of men and women rather than men and women seeking the face of God, and reflect a God-ordained spirituality under his sovereignty and not our own control or by our own self-effort. Their ultimate goal is to help us learn "to love with God's love and . . . serve with God's power."[107] Such authentic disciplines include suffering and painful experiences that help us to become more like Jesus,[108] and they are similar to the highly stressful life events and trauma that lead to perceived growth that has been described as "posttraumatic growth", "stress-related growth", and "benefit-finding."[109] Biblical meaning making and benefit-finding can be part of helping clients

---

103. Calhoun, *Spiritual Disciplines Handbook.*

104. Plummer, "Are the Spiritual Disciplines of 'Silence and Solitude' Really Biblical?"

105. Thomas, *Authentic Faith*; Tang, "Not Just for Monks."

106. Thomas, *Authentic Faith.*

107. Thomas, *Authentic Faith*, 16.

108. Burns, "Embracing Weakness"; Coe, "Musings on the Dark Night of the Soul."

109. Helgeson et al., "Meta-Analytic Review of Benefit Finding and Growth"; Park and Helgeson, "Introduction to the Special Section"; Calhoun and Tedeschi, *Handbook of Posttraumatic Growth*; Calhoun and Tedeschi, *Posttraumatic Growth in Clinical Practice*; Park, "Making Sense of the Meaning Literature"; Park et al., *Trauma, Meaning, and Spirituality.*

process their experiences of authentic disciplines, including pain and suffering.

However, a biblical perspective on suffering and spiritual formation into deeper Christlikeness will go beyond posttraumatic growth and benefit-finding that may be too focused on self-improvement and present benefits and blessings to oneself, to having an eternal perspective on outcomes or results that may not be experienced on earth but only in heaven to come.[110] Furthermore, suffering is not the only or necessary pathway to growth. Recent research has shown that positive and joyful experiences can also lead to growth, called postecstatic growth, and not just posttraumatic growth due to suffering.[111] This more balanced view that both positive, joyful experiences as well as suffering and painful experiences can lead to growth is consistent with Scripture.[112]

The ultimate goal of Christian therapy is not only the alleviation of symptoms but also to deepen spiritual maturity in the client. The appropriate use of spiritual disciplines in a non-legalisitic, grace-filled way, empowered by the Holy Spirit, including growing through authentic disciplines of both suffering and joy and contentment, is a crucial part of explicit integration.[113] This will also involve some degree of spiritual direction, or the process of discerning and surrendering to God's will and deepening one's relationship with God in the context of one's experiences in life by meeting with someone for prayer and spiritual conversation.[114] Ultimately, however, it is the Holy Spirit who transforms us, both therapist and client, into deeper Christlikeness (2 Cor 3:18), and

110. Tan, "Beyond Resilience, Posttraumatic Growth, and Self-Care"; Crabb, *Waiting for Heaven*.

111. Tan, "Is Suffering Necessary for Growth?"; Mangelsdorf et al., "Does Growth Require Suffering."

112. Tan, "Beyond Resilience, Posttraumatic Growth, and Self-Care"; Tan, "Is Suffering Necessary for Growth?."

113. Eck, "Exploration of the Therapeutic Use of Spiritual Disciplines in Clinical Practice" for an exploration of the therapeutic use of 39 spiritual disciplines.

114. Benner, *Sacred Companions*, 94.

not the traditional spiritual disciplines or practices themselves.[115] While some leaders in the Christian therapy field do not advocate integrating spiritual direction into Christian therapy,[116] many others support doing so, including the use of spiritual disciplines in Christian therapy.[117] In fact, psychotherapy itself can be viewed as "work in the Spirit,"[118] or even conceptualized as a spiritual discipline because it is an intentional practice that involves facing our brokenness and being dependent on God's grace, eventually helping us in the sanctification process, for the ultimate purpose of being formed in the image of Christ.[119]

A couple of studies have found that potentially the most efficient way of training therapists to explicitly use religious and spiritual interventions in clinical practice in explicit integration is through intervention-specific training and supervision involving actual clinical experience with religious clients, and not coursework in integration and theology.[120] Christian clinical supervision of actual clinical practice involving explicit integration with Christian clients is therefore crucial in developing therapist integration skills, including the use of Christian spiritual interventions and spiritual disciplines in therapy.[121]

The empirical evidence for the effectiveness of religious and spiritual therapies in general has substantially grown in recent years. The latest review and meta-analysis comprehensively

---

115. Tan, "Holy Spirit and Positive Psychology in Spiritual Formation"; Tan and Gregg, *Disciplines of the Holy Spirit*.

116. McMinn and Campbell, *Integrative Psychotherapy*.

117. Tan, "Integrating Spiritual Direction into Psychotherapy"; Benner, *Intensive Soul Care*; Crabb, *Soultalk*; Moon and Benner, *Spiritual Direction and the Care of Souls*.

118. Kunst and Tan, "Psychotherapy as 'Work in the Spirit.'"

119. White, "Conceptualizing Therapy as a Spiritual Discipline."

120. Walker et al., "Therapists' Use of Religious and Spiritual Interventions in Christian Counseling"; Walker et al., "Use of Religious and Spiritual Interventions by Trainees in APA-Accredited Christian Clinical Programs."

121. Tan, "Developing Integration Skills"; Barto, "Integration of Religious and Spiritual Issues in Clinical Supervision and Implications for Christian Supervisors"; Watson, *Developing Clinicians of Character*.

included 97 outcome studies (N=7,181) on religious and spiritual therapies, including Christian therapies, and found that religious and spiritual therapies had significantly greater improvement in the psychological and spiritual functioning of clients compared to no-treatment and non-religious/ spiritual therapies. In additive studies that are more rigorous, religious and spiritual therapies were found to be as effective as standard approaches in decreasing psychological distress, but led to significantly greater spiritual well-being.[122] The empirical evidence supporting the effectiveness of religious and spiritual therapies, including Christian therapies, is therefore solid and substantial.

More specifically, in an earlier review of empirically supported religious and spiritual therapies in general,[123] the following were considered efficacious treatments: Christian accommodative cognitive therapy for depression and twelve-step facilitation for alcoholism, and Muslim psychotherapy for depression as well as for anxiety when used with medication. Possibly efficacious treatments included: Christian devotional meditation for anxiety, Taoist cognitive therapy for anxiety, Christian accommodative group treatment for unforgiveness, spiritual group treatment for unforgiveness, Christian accommodative group cognitive-behavioral therapy for marital discord, Christian lay counseling for general psychological problems, spiritual group therapy for eating disorders when combined with existing inpatient treatment, and Buddhist accommodative cognitive therapy for anger in a prison setting. Evidence-based practices specifically for Christian counseling and psychotherapy have been described in Worthington et al.[124]

Explicit integration in Christian therapy that includes the appropriate and ethical use of spiritual interventions and resources in therapy and incorporates the process of spiritual direction to

---

122. Captari et al., "Integrating Religion and Spirituality into Psychotherapy"; Hook et al., "Religion and Spirituality."

123. Hook et al., "Empirically Supported Religious and Spiritual Therapies."

124. Worthington et al., *Evidence-Based Practices for Christian Counseling and Psychotherapy.*

a certain degree, therefore has great potential "for deep blessing and greater wholeness and shalom for the client who freely chooses such a psychospiritual therapy that aims toward both psychological and spiritual growth as well as the reduction of psychological distress."[125] Explicit integration, as well as implicit integration, should be conducted in an ethically responsible, clinically sensitive, and professionally competent way for the benefit and well-being of the client.[126] This is Christian therapy that is Christ-centered, biblically-based, and Spirit-filled, with implicit or explicit integration or both, intentionally and prayerfully used in clinical practice.[127]

125. Tan, "Integrating Spiritual Direction into Psychotherapy," 20.

126. Tan, "Religion in Clinical Practice."

127. Tan, *Counseling and Psychotherapy.*

3

THE ROLE OF THE HOLY SPIRIT IN CHRISTIAN COUNSELING AND PSYCHOTHERAPY

Abstract: This third and final lecture will briefly cover the person and work of the Holy Spirit as the third person of the Trinity or Triune God (Father, Son, and Holy Spirit). It will focus on the power and gifts, truth, and fruit of the Holy Spirit, and the role of the Holy Spirit in the process of Christian counseling and psychotherapy that is crucial, central, and comprehensive in at least five ways.

In this third and final lecture, I will cover the crucial, central, and comprehensive role of the Holy Spirit in Christian counseling and psychotherapy,[1] and also in Christian spiritual formation.[2]

---

1. Tan, "Holy Spirit"; Tan, *Counseling and Psychotherapy*.

2. Chandler, *Holy Spirit and Christian Formation*; Tan, *Shepherding God's People*; Tan, "Holy Spirit and Positive Psychology in Spiritual Formation"; Barbeau and Jones, *Spirit of God*; Collicut, *Psychology of Christian Character Formation*; Fee, "On Getting the Spirit Back into Spirituality"; Greenman and Kalantzis, *Life in the Spirit*.

The Holy Spirit is the third person of the Trinity or Triune God (Father, Son, and Holy Spirit). Much has been written on the Holy Spirit from a theological perspective (pneumatology) and numerous books are now available.[3] There is also a growing literature on the ministry of the Holy Spirit in the context of Christian therapy and personality functioning, both in articles,[4] as well as in books.[5] I want to especially mention Geoffrey Sutton's most recent book on counseling and psychotherapy with Pentecostal and charismatic Christians, covering culture and research, and assessment and practice.[6]

The crucial role of the Holy Spirit in Christian counseling and psychotherapy is supported in Scripture that describes the Holy Spirit as the Counselor, Comforter, Helper, or Advocate (John 14:16–17). As Adams has pointed out, at least three persons are involved in every counseling situation: the counselor, the client or counselee, and the Holy Spirit who is the Counselor par excellence.[7] The Nicene Creed describes the Holy Spirit as the

3. Allison and Kostenberger, *Holy Spirit*; Burke and Warrington, *Biblical Theology of the Holy Spirit*; Cole, *He Who Gives Life*; Crisp and Sanders, *Third Person of the Trinity*; Fee, *God's Empowering Presence*; Habets, *Progressive Mystery*; Horton, *Rediscovering the Holy Spirit*; Karkkainen, *Pneumatology*; Levering, *Engaging the Doctrine of the Holy Spirit*; Levison, *Filled with the Spirit*; Levison, *Inspired*; Levison, *Boundless God*; Levison, *Unconventional God*; Moltmann, *Source of Life*; Packer, *Keep in Step with the Spirit*; Pinnock, *Flame of Love*; Thiselton, *Holy Spirit*; Yong, *Spirit of Love*.

4. Coe, "Beyond Relationality to Union"; Dodds, "Role of the Holy Spirit in Personality Growth and Change"; Ingram, "Psychological Aspects of the Filling of the Holy Spirit"; Kunst and Tan, "Psychotherapy as 'Work in the Spirit'"; Parker, "Winnicott's Object Relations Theory and the Work of the Holy Spirit"; Decker, "Holy Spirit in Counseling"; Hathaway, "Spiritual Gift Inventories"; Tan, "Cultural Issues in Spirit-Filled Psychotherapy."

5. Coe and Hall, *Psychology in the Spirit*; Gilbert and Brock, *Holy Spirit and Counseling Volume 1*; Gilbert and Brock, *Holy Spirit and Counseling Volume 2*; Pugh, *Christian Formation Counseling*; Sutton, *Counseling and Psychotherapy with Pentecostal and Charismatic Christians*; Vining, *Pentecostal Caregivers*; Vining, *Spirit-Centered Counseling*; Vining and Decker, *Soul Care*.

6. Sutton, *Counseling and Psychotherapy with Pentecostal and Charismatic Christians*.

7. Adams, *Christian Counselor's Manual*.

giver of life, based on both the Old Testament and the New Testament.[8] His key role in Christian counseling and therapy as the Counselor as well as giver of life, means that Christian counselors and therapists need to prayerfully depend on the Spirit's presence and healing power in every counseling situation or session, with a basic understanding of the work and ministry of the Holy Spirit.[9]

THE WORK AND MINISTRY OF THE HOLY SPIRIT

The person and work of the Holy Spirit are crucial and essential in our lives and ministries, including pastoral ministry and counseling,[10] and we need to be sensitive and open to the Spirit.[11] The Holy Spirit's power and presence can be accessed and experienced through the traditional spiritual disciplines as power connectors to the Spirit as means of grace,[12] as well as through authentic disciplines or circumstantial spiritual disciplines as mentioned in my previous second lecture.[13] However, the Holy Spirit is sovereign as God, and can work in his own spontaneous and mysterious ways to anoint us with his power, anytime, anywhere, and in any way he wants to, even without us doing anything like practicing the traditional spiritual disciplines! The Holy Spirit as God, is everywhere and has worked in all types of situations and circumstances, with and in all kinds of people, including all of creation, throughout the centuries and all ages of history.[14] The Holy Spirit has been described as God in us, God with us, and God

8. Parker, "Winnicott's Object Relations Theory and the Work of the Holy Spirit," 286; Cole, *He Who Gives Life*; Levison, *Filled with the Spirit*; Levison, *Inspired*; Levison, *Boundless God*; Levison, *Unconventional God*.

9. Tan, "Holy Spirit"; Tan, *Counseling and Psychotherapy*.

10. Tan, *Shepherding God's People*, 14–23.

11. McKnight, *Open to the Spirit*; Storms, *Practicing the Power*.

12. Tan and Gregg, *Disciplines of the Holy Spirit*.

13. Thomas, *Authentic Faith*; Tan, *Full Service*.

14. Levison, *Filled with the Spirit*; Levison, *Inspired*; Levison, *Boundless God*; Levison, *Unconventional God*; Thiselton, *Holy Spirit*.

transforming us, as the One who transforms and transcends our human abilities.[15]

The Holy Spirit's presence and power are essential in our lives and ministries, including counseling and psychotherapy that can be viewed as "work in the Spirit,"[16] and even as a spiritual discipline.[17] Scripture strongly states that it is "'not by might nor by power, but by my Spirit,' says the Lord Almighty" (Zech 4:6) that his work is accomplished. Jesus himself definitively asserted that "apart from me you can do nothing" (John 15:5), and in Eph 5:18, we are commanded to "be [continually] filled with the Spirit," again and again. We are not to grieve the Spirit (Eph 4:30) with the sins of the flesh or sinful nature (such as bitterness, rage and anger, brawling, slander, and malice) and not to quench the Spirit or put out his fire (1 Thess 5:19) with unbelief or evil. We therefore need to yield to the Holy Spirit and ask to be filled with the Spirit through prayer, for him to take control of our lives and anoint us with his presence and power. The following is a brief prayer that may be helpful for those of us who desire to be filled with the Spirit (Eph 5:18), and to ask for him to empower us to become more like Jesus in our character and in our ministries, including counseling and psychotherapy: "Dear Father, I come to you and ask in the Name of Jesus for you to cleanse me and fill me with the Holy Spirit and his power and presence, so that I can become more like Jesus in my life and ministries, including counseling and psychotherapy. Thank you so much. In Jesus' Name, Amen!"[18]

As mentioned earlier, the Holy Spirit is sovereign, and he can work in his own spontaneous and even mysterious ways his wonders to perform, including anointing us afresh with his presence and power or fire from above, all by God's sheer grace and goodness and generosity, even without us taking any formulaic steps or doing anything such as practicing the traditional spiritual disciplines. Anthony Thiselton has highlighted the "ascending" ministry of the

15. McKnight, *Open to the Spirit.*

16. Kunst and Tan, "Psychotherapy as 'Work in the Spirit.'"

17. White, "Conceptualizing Therapy as a Spiritual Discipline."

18. Tan, *Shepherding God's People,* 18.

Spirit in initiating and inspiring prayer, worship, and thanksgiving, as being as important as and parallel to his "descending" work of inspiration and empowerment.[19] We need the help and ministry of the Holy Spirit even in the practice of spiritual disciplines such as prayer and worship. We therefore serve the Lord in dependence on the Lord and the power of the Holy Spirit, and not by our own self-effort centered in our individual giftings, skills, competence, or methods. Ultimately, it is the Holy Spirit as the Spirit of Love who empowers us to love God and others, including our enemies, and to manifest that love as the fruit of the Spirit (Gal 5:22–23) in our lives and service to others, even unto death if need be, in following Jesus all the way.[20] Rom 5:5 states: "And hope does not put us to shame, because God's love has been poured out into our hearts through the Holy Spirit, who has been given to us."

Tan and Gregg, in *Disciplines of the Holy Spirit*, delineated the following blessings or results of the Spirit-filled life: "greater love and intimacy with God; exaltation of Jesus as Son of God and Savior; power and boldness to witness and preach; greater wisdom and faith; deep joy (singing and worship); release of spiritual gifts for ministry; victory over sin and temptation; effectiveness and power through prayer; quiet confidence during opposition; deeper trust in Scripture as the Word of God; renewed zeal for evangelism; and fresh love of Christ and others."[21] The Holy Spirit can at times also lead us, as he led Jesus, into the wilderness to encounter temptations and spiritual warfare, and sometimes even experience dark nights of the soul (see Matt 4:1; Luke 4:1–2). The filling of the Spirit can result in both dramatic external manifestations, including speaking in tongues (see Acts 2:1–4; 10:44–47; 19:1–7), as well as relatively less dramatic and more quiet manifestations such as boldness in preaching or witnessing, deeper faith and wisdom, and joy (Acts 4:8, 31; 6:3, 5; 11:24; 13:52). The Holy Spirit will also help us to pray in the Spirit (see Rom 8:26; Eph 6:18; Jude 20; see also Heb 5:7) on all occasions and with all kinds of prayers (e.g., with

19. Thiselton, *Holy Spirit*, 500.

20. Yong, *Spirit of Love*, 160.

21. Tan and Gregg, *Disciplines of the Holy Spirit*, 21.

words or without words including wordless groans, with tongues or without tongues, with tears or without tears, with lament or praise and thanksgiving in worship and awe, with confession and requests of all kinds in petition for self and intercession for others).

I will now cover, in more detail, three major ways in which the work and ministry of the Holy Spirit can be further described from a biblical perspective: the Spirit's power and gifts, the Spirit's truth, and the Spirit's fruit, all of which are particularly relevant and helpful in Christian counseling and psychotherapy.[22]

The Spirit's Power and Gifts

The power of the Holy Spirit is essential in evangelism and witnessing (Acts 1:8), and other ministries such as pastoral and church ministries, as well as counseling.[23] We need to be continually filled with the Spirit (Eph 5:18) on a daily, moment by moment basis, as we walk in or by the Spirit (Gal 5:16) so we do not give in to the desires of the flesh or sinful nature, and keep in step with the Spirit by faith as we live by the Spirit, the giver of life and power (Gal 5:25). As we prayerfully surrender to the Spirit and ask specifically for his filling, he empowers us and helps us to become more like Jesus and to do the works of Jesus in our service and ministries, including Christian counseling and psychotherapy.[24] The Holy Spirit often works by sovereignly and supernaturally manifesting himself through spiritual gifts which are described as a "manifestation" of the Holy Spirit in 1 Cor 12:7. Sam Storms puts it this way: "*The gifts are God himself working in and through us.* They are concrete, often tangible, visible and vocal disclosures of divine power showcased through human activity. A *charism* or gift of the Spirit is the Holy Spirit himself coming to clear and sometimes dramatic expression in the lives of God's people as they minister to one another."[25]

---

22. Tan, "Holy Spirit," 568; Tan, *Counseling and Psychotherapy*.

23. Tan, *Shepherding God's People*.

24. Hayford, "Spirit-Formed in Purity and Power."

25. Storms, *Practicing the Power*, 15 (emphasis in the original).

There are various listings and descriptions of spiritual gifts, conventionally understood, and a well-known list, with an accompanying spiritual gifts inventory, has been provided and described by Peter Wagner, with the following twenty eight spiritual gifts based on Scripture (e.g., see Rom 12; 1 Cor 12; Eph 4; 1 Pet 4): prophecy, service, teaching, exhortation, giving, leadership, mercy, wisdom, knowledge, faith, healing, miracles, discerning of spirits, tongues, interpretation of tongues, apostle, helps, administration, evangelist, pastor, celibacy, voluntary poverty, martyrdom, hospitality, missionary, intercession, deliverance, and leading worship.[26] There are other authors who have interpreted spiritual gifts not as special *abilities* given by the Holy Spirit to us (the conventional view) but instead as different *ministries* that the Holy Spirit calls us to serve in, in order to build up the body of Christ or the church.[27]

However we view spiritual gifts, whether traditionally as special abilities given by the Spirit, or as different ministries also given by the Spirit, spiritual gifts are droplets of grace from God to empower and enable us to be faithful and fruitful in whatever ministries he has called us to serve in, to glorify God and bless others for eternity. We receive these spiritual gifts from the Spirit with gratitude, love, and humility, as we serve God and others, including in the ministry of Christian counseling and psychotherapy. Spiritual gifts that may be especially helpful for an effective counseling ministry include: exhortation or encouragement (Rom 12:8); healing (1 Cor 12:9, 28); wisdom or a word of wisdom (1 Cor 12:8); knowledge or a word of knowledge (1 Cor 12:8); discerning of spirits (1 Cor 12:10); and mercy (Rom 12:8).[28] Other spiritual gifts that may be viewed as important and relevant for counseling ministries, especially from a Pentecostal or charismatic perspective include prophecy, teaching, faith, miracles, tongues, and intercession. Hathaway recently reviewed several spiritual gift inventories and their validity and function, and reported their lack

---

26. Hathaway, "Spiritual Gift Inventories"; Wagner, *Your Spiritual Gifts Can Help Your Church Grow*.

27. Aker, "Charismata"; Berding, *What are Spiritual Gifts?*.

28. Tan, "Holy Spirit," 568; Tan, *Counseling and Psychotherapy*.

of validity and other important psychometric properties.[29] Great care and caution should therefore be exercised in the use of spiritual gift inventories due to the danger or risk of misinterpreting or over interpreting them.

The Spirit's Truth

The Holy Spirit is the Spirit of truth, and he will teach us and guide us into all truth (John 14:16–17, 26; 16:13). This includes psycho-theological truth that is central and salient in all integration endeavors, including in the context of counseling and psychotherapy. Such eternal truth is ultimately what will set us free (John 8:32), centered in Jesus Christ who is the Truth (John 14:6), and the Way and the Life. The Holy Spirit inspired the writing of Scripture as God's Word (2 Tim 3:16; 2 Pet 1:20–21). He will guide us as Christian counselors and psychotherapists to use Scripture in our clinical practice in empathic, compassionate, sensitive, wise, and deeply helpful ways with our clients, bringing healing and wholeness or shalom to them in the midst of their pain and struggles in life. However, the Holy Spirit will never contradict the eternal truth of Scripture or God's inspired Word, properly interpreted and illuminated with his help. He will always uphold the veracity and validity of Scripture in all areas of life and ministry, including the counseling and therapy context, being consistent with the moral and ethical aspects of biblical truth and teaching.

The Spirit's Fruit

The Holy Spirit also produces the fruit of the Spirit mentioned in Gal 5:22–23, that refers mainly and basically to Christlike love or *agape* that is the hallmark of mature Christlikeness (Rom 8:29; Gal 4:19) in genuine Christian spiritual formation. The fruit of the Spirit is: love, joy, peace, forbearance (patience), kindness, goodness, faithfulness, gentleness, and self-control (Gal 5:22–23). Such

29. Hathaway, "Spiritual Gift Inventories."

Christlike fruit cannot be faked or manufactured by ourselves or our own self-efforts, but it can only be produced or brought forth by the Holy Spirit within us, as we abide and remain in Christ (John 15:5). This agape love from the Spirit of love,[30] is powerfully therapeutic and healing in counseling ministries and in the therapeutic process and relationship with the client. It is also essential in all other pastoral and church ministries, for without love we are nothing and have achieved nothing (1 Cor 13).[31]

All these major aspects of the Holy Spirit's work and ministry (power, truth, and love) that are crucial and essential should exist and function together in biblical balance. Power without love can result in abuse. Power without truth can lead to heresy. However, power rooted in biblical truth and appropriately and gently used with Christlike love can be deeply therapeutic and bring healing and wholeness to clients in the brokenness and pain of their lives. It can also lead to renewal and revival![32]

THE WORK OF THE HOLY SPIRIT IN COUNSELING AND PSYCHOTHERAPY

The Holy Spirit can work in various and different ways in his sovereign and healing ministry during a counseling or therapy session, in both implicit and explicit integration in clinical practice. In more implicit integration approaches to therapy (e.g., psychodynamic or psychoanalytic therapy), the Holy Spirit's work as giver of life may be emphasized more such as Parker has done in his description of the Spirit's creative work in therapy that makes use of Winnicott's object relations theory and the concepts of transitional phenomena and object usage.[33] The Spirit can touch clients

30. Yong, *Spirit of Love*; Pinnock, *Flame of Love*.

31. Tan, *Shepherding God's People*, 21.

32. Tan, "Holy Spirit and Positive Psychology in Spiritual Formation"; Tan, *Counseling and Psychotherapy*.

33. Parker, "Winnicott's Object Relations Theory and the Work of the Holy Spirit"; Winnicott, *The Maturational Processes and the Facilitating Environment*; Winnicott, *Playing and Reality*.

by "conferring a sense of identity and providing an environment for emergence of a strong spiritual self . . . and in engendering new life by making God real in ways that transcend our imaginings."[34] The life-giving work of the Holy Spirit also helps a client to hold on to a basic sense of hope even when all the client's "wishes, dreams, disappointments, fears, and frustrations have been spent,"[35] by making God real to the client in the midst of subjectively experiencing the absence of God.

The Holy Spirit can similarly work in implicit integration that is intentional and incarnational, as in relational psychodynamic therapy,[36] object relations therapy,[37] and relational psychoanalysis.[38] The Spirit's work in these therapy sessions is quietly but intentionally and prayerfully embraced and expressed by the Christian therapist and experienced by the client in the empathy and agape love of the Spirit in the therapeutic process and relationship. The deep but quiet work of the Spirit is manifested in the transcendent moments and creative experiences in implicit integration rather than in more explicit and overt ways such as the verbal use of prayer and Scripture and other spiritual resources. Psychotherapy in these implicit but intentional and incarnational approaches, is still "work in the Spirit" because the Holy Spirit is at work in more reflective and quiet ways.[39] John Pugh has pointed out that the Holy Spirit works in and through the daily "awful experiences of human existence."[40]

The Holy Spirit can also work in explicit integration approaches in Christian counseling and psychotherapy that more

34. Parker, "Winnicott's Object Relations Theory and the Work of the Holy Spirit," 292.

35. Parker, "Winnicott's Object Relations Theory and the Work of the Holy Spirit," 292.

36. Terrell, "Discussion of Intentional Incarnational Integration in Relational Psychodynamic Psychotherapy."

37. Rogers, "Where the Moment Meets the Transcendent."

38. Bland and Strawn, *Christianity and Psychoanalysis*; Hoffman, *Toward Mutual Recognition*.

39. Kunst and Tan, "Psychotherapy as 'Work in the Spirit.'"

40. Pugh, *Christian Formation Counseling, 280*.

overtly and systematically use spiritual resources such as prayer and Scripture and other spiritual disciplines, and more directly and verbally deal with spiritual and religious issues, in therapy sessions with clients. While the Holy Spirit can work in whatever way at whatever time with whoever and through whoever he wants to, there are at least five ways that he can work during a therapy session, especially in a more explicit integration approach to therapy.[41]

First, the Holy Spirit can directly empower or enable the Christian therapist to discern the root problems of the client more accurately and perhaps more quickly, by giving relevant and specific words of knowledge or wisdom (1 Cor 12:8) to the Christian therapist in assessing and helping the client. Swindoll has described such experiences of receiving words of knowledge or wisdom from the Spirit as "inner promptings" or nudges of the Spirit within the Christian counselor who is prayerfully attentive to the Spirit's leading, from a more conservative evangelical perspective.[42] These promptings or words of knowledge or wisdom from the Spirit can also enable the Christian counselor to more deeply engage in spiritual conversation with the client or "soultalk" as Crabb puts it.[43] "Flash prayers" can be quietly used by a Christian therapist during a counseling or therapy session to be more mindfully attentive to the Holy Spirit and his presence and power, for example: "Spirit of God, please guide me"; "Holy Spirit, please minister to the client with your healing grace"; "Holy Spirit, help us at this point of being stuck"; "Holy Spirit, comfort and strengthen the client"; "Spirit of God, protect us and empower us"; "Holy Spirit, have mercy on us." This can also occur in more implicit integration approaches such as relational psychodynamic or psychanalytic therapy. The Holy Spirit will help us to pray in the Spirit (Eph 6:18, Jude 20), often with wordless groans or groanings within us (Rom 8:26).

---

41. Tan, "Holy Spirit"; Tan, *Counseling and Psychotherapy.*

42. Swindoll, "Helping and the Holy Spirit"; Deere, *Surprised by the Power of the Spirit*; Deere, *Surprised by the Voice of God.*

43. Crabb, *Soultalk.*

Second, the Holy Spirit can provide clear spiritual direction regarding God's will to both the Christian therapist and the client as they engage in more explicit integration practices during a therapy session, including praying together, using and discussing Scripture, and openly dealing with spiritual issues and struggles. As already mentioned, the Spirit can also do this and provide clear guidance and spiritual direction during a counseling session, in more implicit integration approaches.

Third, the Holy Spirit can directly minister to and deeply touch a client in powerful ways with his healing grace and transforming power. This experience can happen anytime according to God's sovereign grace and goodness, and the supernatural ministry of the Spirit, sometimes leading to sudden insights and epiphanies that result in deep transformation of ordinary lives, or what has been described as "quantum change."[44] These transcendent moments, including quantum change experiences can however be helpfully facilitated by the explicit use of prayer, including inner healing prayer or healing of memories.[45] The direct touch of the Spirit in transcendent and creative moments in a therapy session can also occur in more implicit integration approaches to therapy.

Fourth, the Holy Spirit can enable the Christian therapist to discern the presence of the demonic or whether there is demonization or demonic oppression in the client's life. He can more specifically give the Christian therapist the spiritual gift of discerning of spirits or distinguishing between spirits (1 Cor 12:10), which can be especially helpful in making an accurate differential diagnosis between demonization and mental disorder, or a dual diagnosis of both demonization and mental disorder co-existing in a client. The Holy Spirit can also empower the Christian therapist to deal effectively and victoriously over the demonic, if it is present, by helping the therapist to pray effective prayers for deliverance and protection from the demonic, if this is necessary and appropriate, with full informed consent and collaboration from the client.

44. Miller and C'de Baca, *Quantum Change.*

45. Tan, "Inner Healing Prayer"; Tan, "Use of Prayer and Scripture in Cognitive-Behavioral Therapy"; Garzon and Burkett, "Healing of Memories."

Usually, however, it may be more appropriate to refer the client with possible demonization to a deliverance specialist, or pastor, or deliverance prayer ministry team experienced in deliverance work, preferably within the client's own denomination or church.[46]

Fifth, and finally, the Holy Spirit can work deeply in the Christian spiritual formation into deeper Christlikeness (Rom 8:29; Gal 4:19) of both the client and therapist, as they engage in the practice of the traditional spiritual disciplines (e.g., solitude and silence, listening and guidance, prayer and intercession, study and meditation, repentance and confession, yielding and submission, fasting, worship, fellowship, simplicity, service, and witness) in the power of the Spirit as well as reflect on and discuss growing and meaning-making through the authentic disciplines or circumstantial spiritual disciplines that are not usually within our control or choice, such as suffering, waiting, mourning, sacrifice, persecution, contentment, and hope and fear.[47] Some of these spiritual disciplines can be practiced or discussed in the therapy session, while others can be assigned as homework tasks to be completed by the client in between therapy sessions. They can help both the therapist and client to more deeply experience the Spirit's presence and power for the client's growth and healing. It is the Holy Spirit however who ultimately brings about deep spiritual and psychological transformation, whether implicitly or explicitly, in the client, as well as in the therapist.[48] This is the sovereign work of God and by his grace alone, so that the Spirit can work in any way

46. Appleby, *It's Only a Demon*; Appleby, "Deliverance as Part of the Therapeutic Process"; Bufford, *Counseling and the Demonic*; MacNutt, *Deliverance from Evil Spirits*.

47. Tan and Gregg, *Disciplines of the Holy Spirit*; Thomas, *Authentic Faith*; Tan, *Full Service*.

48. Coe and Hall, *Psychology in the Spirit*; Collicutt, *Psychology of Christian Character Formation*; Eck, "Exploration of the Therapeutic Use of Spiritual Disciplines in Clinical Practice"; Gaultiere and Gaultiere, *Journey of the Soul*; Barbeau and Jones, *Spirit of God*; Chan, "Introduction to the Special Theme"; Chandler, *Holy Spirit and Christian Formation*; Fee, "On Getting the Spirit Back into Spirituality"; Greenman and Kalantzis, *Life in the Spirit*; Tan, *Shepherding God's People*; Tan, "Holy Spirit and Positive Psychology in Spiritual Formation."

he wants to even without or apart from the spiritual disciplines. It is, therefore, also not totally true to say that a therapist can lead a client to go or grow only as far as the therapist has, spiritually or psychologically. The Holy Spirit can and often will bring both of them beyond their current levels of functioning and growth! To God alone be the glory for the deep and wonderful things he has done, by his grace alone!

It will be helpful for us to keep in mind the meaning of genuine Christian spiritual formation into deeper Christlikeness, using the following biblically-based and theologically oriented succinct definition by Jeffrey Greenman: "Spiritual formation is our continuing response to the reality of God's grace shaping us into the likeness of Christ, through the work of the Holy Spirit, in the community of faith, for the sake of the world."[49]

The work of the Holy Spirit in Christian counseling and psychotherapy is therefore crucial, central, and comprehensive in bringing about deep and genuine growth and healing, psychologically and spiritually, in the client, and as a side-effect, in the therapist too in what has been called the "helper therapy" principle.[50] Although training and competence in therapy skills are needed, Christian therapists will use such skills in dependence on the Holy Spirit as the *Counselor par excellence*, in their clinical training, practice, and supervision. A Christian approach to counseling and psychotherapy will therefore be Christ-centered, biblically-based, and Spirit-filled, to the glory of God, and the blessing and healing of persons including both the client and the therapist. A Christian therapist so led and filled with the Spirit can relax and rest more in the Lord, as the hard and deep work of counseling and therapy is done in the power and presence of the Spirit, in dependence on God's grace.

49. Greenman, "Spiritual Formation in Theological Perspective," 24.
50. Reissman, "'Helper Therapy' Principle."

CONCLUDING COMMENTS

In this series of three lectures for the 2021 Fuller Integration Symposium, I have spoken on the overall theme of "A Christian approach to counseling and psychotherapy: Christ-centered, biblically-based, and Spirit-filled." I have attempted to deal with this topic as broadly as possible, both from theological and psychological perspectives. It is nevertheless still a Christian approach, not the one and only Christian approach!

I would like to end with several concluding comments.[51] First, as Christian therapists, we need to have faith or trust in Jesus Christ as Lord of all our professional and academic disciplines, including psychology and counseling or psychotherapy.[52] As Spirit-filled, biblically-based and Christ-centered servants of Jesus Christ, Christian therapists will have faith and full confidence in Christ as the most brilliant person in the universe who is also both master and maestro of every field or discipline of study, including counseling and psychotherapy.[53]

Second, Christian therapists who practice a Christ-centered, biblically-based, and Spirit-filled approach to counseling and psychotherapy by faith, will experience the eternal kind of life that Jesus came to give us (John 3:16, 10:10), and also help their clients to experience such authentic life. Dallas Willard years ago wrote, in this context, the following still relevant and powerful words:

> Many counselors today are learning that for their own work, deep immersion in the disciplines is necessary, both for developing their own character, and beyond that, accessing special powers of grace for their work in counseling people. Many psychologists are learning how to use techniques of prayer and various kinds of ministry to have a much greater effect then they could have if all they had to go on were just the things they learned in their clinical training programs . . . I think the most

51. Tan, *Counseling and Psychotherapy*.

52. Johnson, "Christ, the Lord of Psychology."

53. Tan, "Faith in Psychology and Counseling"; Willard, *Divine Conspiracy*, 95; Willard, *Great Ommission*.

important and the most solid way is to begin to integrate prayer and spiritual teaching into the therapy process as it seems appropriate . . . I think the issue here lies deeper than even matters of integration as we commonly discuss it. It is a matter of our understanding of the gospel of Jesus Christ as one which breaks through the natural world and brings it into the spiritual world and invites us as individuals to learn to live an eternal kind of life now.[54]

Third, I would like us to note that over four decades ago, two prominent leaders in the field of secular psychotherapy, Jerome Frank and Isaac Marks,[55] had already issued a challenge to psychotherapy researchers to give more attention to the role of "healing power" or faith healing involving faith and religious processes, in psychotherapy, and its possible effects on therapeutic outcomes. Although there is now strong and solid empirical evidence supporting the effectiveness of religious and spiritual therapies, including Christian therapies,[56] there is still a need for further well controlled outcome research more specifically on religious and spiritual healing interventions, such as Christian inner healing prayer, and their effectiveness in Christian therapy.

The Holy Spirit will enable us and help us to continue to develop and practice a genuinely Christian approach to counseling and psychotherapy that is Christ-centered, biblically-based, and Spirit-filled or Spirit-led. This endeavor will also require active participation in and involvement with a community of Christian scholars and Christian counselors and psychologists, as well as others, as some recent authors in the integration field have emphasized, in relational, embodied, and community-based approaches to integration.[57] It will only be by God's grace and the work of

54. Willard, "Spirituality," 19–20.

55. Frank, "Therapeutic Components Shared by All Psychotherapies"; Marks, "Behavioral Psychotherapy of Adult Neurosis."

56. Captari et al., "Integrating Religion and Spirituality into Psychotherapy"; Hook et al., "Religion and Spirituality."

57. Neff and McMinn, *Embodying Integration*; Sandage and Brown, *Relational Integration of Psychology and Theology*; Strawn and Brown, *Enhancing Christian Life*; Hall and Hall, *Relational Spirituality*; Sorenson, "Tenth Leper";

the Holy Spirit, that we as Christian counselors and therapists will keep the faith or be kept in the faith in him, in our clinical practice, as well as research and theory building.[58]

Finally, I would like to end this third and final lecture on a more personal note. I want to specially thank Tammi Anderson, my assistant at Fuller Theological Seminary who significantly helped me with the word processing and PowerPoint slides for my lectures, for suggesting that I share more personally at some point in these lectures. As I briefly mentioned in my first lecture, I have written a few autobiographical book chapters in which I shared some details of my life and integration journey or pilgrimage as a Christian psychologist and pastor in a more personal, relational, embodied, and communal context.[59] I would like to quote from the personal letter I wrote at the end of my book chapter on my integration journey and reflections as a Christian psychologist and pastor,[60] that contains six core lessons that I have learned in my integration journey, that I trust will be of some help and blessing to you in your own integration journey and pilgrimage of faith in Christ:

> Dear Friend,
>
> I would like to share with you some lessons that I have learned and any wisdom that I may have gained in my integration journey so far as a Christian psychologist and pastor...
>
> First, I would recommend that you set as your first priority your relationship and walk with the Lord, that he will always be your first love (Rev 2:4) and that you will love him with all your heart, soul, mind, and strength, and love your neighbor as yourself (Mark 12:29–31). The grace-filled practice of the spiritual disciplines on a regular basis will be essential, including a daily quiet time

Sorenson et al., "National Collaborative Research on how Students Learn Integration."

58. Tan, "Faith in Psychology and Counseling," 67.

59. Tan, "My Pilgrimage as a Christian Psychologist"; Tan, "Psychology Collaborating with the Church"; Tan, "My Integration Journey."

60. Tan, "My Integration Journey."

alone with the Lord . . . and periodic longer personal retreats with him for a day or two or longer. Practicing the presence of God throughout the day, for example by using flash prayers often, will also help much. It is out of such deep and intimate relationship with the Lord that you will come to know and understand truth more fully, including the psychotheological truth that is foundational for all good integration—that is, for all integration that is Christ-centered, Bible-based, and Spirit- filled.

Second, I want to thank God for the many mentors, formal or informal, whom he has graciously sent into my life . . . I have learned so much from them. I wish some of my earlier mentors had taught me more firmly the need to set limits and to not take on too much, as well as to live a more balanced life with adequate rest and sleep, good nutrition, and regular exercise. May you learn these precious lessons early on in your integration journey. I pray and wish for you to have a few good mentors, especially humble, loving, and Christlike Christian mentors, who will provide the loving support, intellectual stimulation, rigorous challenge, spiritual direction, and faithful prayers for you in your integration journey.

Third, there is much helpful literature that is now available on the integration of Christian faith and psychology, including therapy, that is essential reading for you . . . Recent work on developing a distinctively Christian psychology that is more substantially grounded in biblical and historical theology, as well as in Scripture itself is also required reading for you and me. In this regard, it is of ultimate importance and value to be saturated with Scripture as the inspired, eternal word of God (2 Tim 3:16).

Fourth, learn to be filled daily with the power and presence of the Holy Spirit (Eph 5:18), by confession of sins and by yielding to him and the Lordship of Christ. Each day in prayer, ask him to anoint you afresh with his wisdom, truth, power, and love, as well as with the spiritual gifts that will equip you to be a more faithful and fruitful servant of Jesus Christ, capable of doing good integration work. Be prayerfully dependent on the Holy Spirit, who is the Counselor or Comforter par excellence

(John 14:16–17), especially in clinical practice or therapy with clients, where his agape love can be manifested in a warm, empathic, and genuine therapeutic relationship with clients.

Fifth, be thankful for how we are wounded healers ourselves . . . remember that God can use your own sufferings and struggles to expand and deepen your capacity for empathy and compassionate caring, as manifested in the form of agape love that you can share with your clients and with others who are suffering (2 Cor 1:3–4). Gratitude . . . will also help you experience growth through trials and struggles, seeing them as opportunities to become more Christlike and spiritually mature, rather than seeing them as hindrances.

Finally I would like to suggest that you do not make psychology, therapy, or even the integration task to be everything in your life . . . instead, seek the Lord and his kingdom first (Matt 6:33), and always see the bigger picture of God's will and God's kingdom with loving obedience to him . . . This means living the eternal kind of life, a life in the kingdom, where he rules and reigns over every area of your life and mine. It includes . . . enough time for yourself and your family, as well as time for the church as a loving community of faith and as the larger family of God. And . . . it includes enough time to reach out to others, especially the lost, the oppressed, and the broken –reaching out with the good news of Jesus Christ, who alone can ultimately save us all.

I would like to wish you the Lord's best and deepest blessings, as you walk on with him in your integration journey. God Bless!

With his love and prayers, Warmly, Siang-Yang Tan.[61]

61. Tan, "My Integration Journey," 86–88.

BIBLIOGRAPHY

Adams, Jay. *The Christian Counselor's Manual.* Grand Rapids: Baker Academic, 1973.

———. *Competent to Counsel.* Grand Rapids: Baker Academic, 1970.

Aker, Benny. "Charismata: Gifts, Enablements, or Ministries?" *Journal of Pentecostal Theology* 11 (2002) 53–69.

Allison, Greg, and Andreas Kostenberger. *The Holy Spirit.* Nashville: B & H Academic, 2020.

Alsdurf, Jim, and H. Newton Malony. "A Critique of Ruth Carter Stapleton's Ministry of 'Inner Healing.'" *Journal of Psychology and Theology* 8 (1980) 173–84.

Anderson, Neil, et al. *Christ-Centered Therapy: The Practical Integration of Theology and Psychology.* Grand Rapids: Zondervan, 2000.

Appleby, David. "Deliverance as Part of the Therapeutic Process." In *Transformative Encounters: The Intervention of God in Christian Counseling and Pastoral Care,* edited by David Appleby and George Ohlschlager, 77–93. Downers Grove, IL: IVP Academic, 2013.

———. *It's Only a Demon: A Model of Christian Deliverance.* Winona Lake, IN: BMH, 2009.

Appleby, David, and George Ohlschlager, eds. *Transformative Encounters: The Intervention of God in Christian Counseling and Pastoral Care.* Downers Grove, IL: IVP Academic, 2013.

Arterburn, Stephen, and Jack Felton. *Toxic Faith: Understanding and Overcoming Religious Addiction.* Nashville: Thomas Nelson, 1991.

Aten, Jamie, and Mark Leach, eds. *Spirituality and the Therapeutic Process: A Comprehensive Resource from Intake to Termination.* Washington, DC: American Psychological Association, 2009.

Aten, Jamie, et al., eds. *Spiritually Oriented Interventions for Counseling and Psychotherapy.* Washington, DC: American Psychological Association, 2011.

Backus, William. *Telling the Truth to Troubled People.* Minneapolis: Bethany House, 1985.

Backus, William, and Marie Chapian. *Telling Yourself the Truth*. Minneapolis: Bethany House, 1980.

Bade, Mary, and Stephen Cook. "Functions of Christian Prayer in the Coping Process." *Journal for the Scientific Study of Religion* 47 (2008) 123–33.

Balswick, Jack, et al. *The Reciprocating Self: Human Development in Theological Perspective*. 2nd ed. Downers Grove, IL: IVP Academic, 2016.

Barbeau, Jeffery, and Beth Jones, eds. *Spirit of God: Christian Renewal in the Community of Faith*. Downers Grove, IL: IVP Academic, 2015.

Barto, Heather. "The Integration of Religious and Spiritual Issues in Clinical Supervision and Implications for Christian Supervisors." *Journal of Psychology and Christianity* 37 (2018) 235–46.

Beck, James, and Bruce Demarest. *The Human Person in Theology and Psychology: A Biblical Anthropology for the Twenty-First Century*. Grand Rapids: Kregel, 2005.

Benner, David. "Intensive Soul Care: Integrating Psychotherapy and Spiritual Direction." In *Spiritually Oriented Psychotherapy*, edited by Len Sperry and Edward Shafranske, 287–306. Washington, DC: American Psychological Association, 2005.

————. *Sacred Companions: The Gift of Spiritual Friendship and Direction*. Downers Grove, IL: InterVarsity, 2002.

Bennett, Kyle. *Practices of Love: Spiritual Disciplines for the Life of the World*. Grand Rapids: Brazos, 2017.

Berding, Kenneth. *What are Spiritual Gifts? Rethinking the Conventional View*. Grand Rapids: Kregel, 2006.

Bland, Earl, and Brad Strawn. "A New Conversation." In *Christianity and Psychoanalysis: A New Conversation*, edited by Earl Bland and Brad Strawn, 13–35. Downers Grove, IL: IVP Academic, 2014.

————, eds. *Christianity and Psychoanalysis: A New Conversation*. Downers Grove, IL: IVP Academic, 2014.

Blanton, P. Gregg. *Contemplation and Counseling: An Integrative Model for Practitioners*. Downers Grove, IL: IVP Academic, 2019.

Booth, Leo. *When God Becomes a Drug: Breaking the Chains of Religious Addiction and Abuse*. New York: Jeremy P. Tarcher / Pedigree, 1991.

Brown, Warren. "Resonance: A Model for Relating Science, Psychology, and Faith." *Journal of Psychology and Christianity* 23 (2004) 110–20.

Brown, Warren, and Brad Strawn. *The Physical Nature of Christian Life: Neuroscience, Psychology, and the Church*. New York: Cambridge University Press, 2012.

Brown, Warren, et al. *Whatever Happened to the Soul? Scientific and Theological Portraits of Human Nature*. Minneapolis: Fortress, 1998.

Brugger, E. Christian and the Faculty of the Institute for the Psychological Sciences. "Anthropological Foundations for Clinical Psychology: A Proposal." *Journal of Psychology and Theology* 36 (2008) 3–15.

Bufford, Rodger. "Consecrated Counseling. Reflections on the Distinctives of Christian Counseling." *Journal of Psychology and Theology* 25 (1997) 111–22.

———. *Counseling and the Demonic.* Dallas: Word, 1988.

Burke, Trevor, and Keith Warrington, eds. *A Biblical Theology of the Holy Spirit.* Eugene: Cascade, 2014.

Burns, Scott. "Embracing Weakness: An Investigation of the Role of Weakness in Spiritual Growth." *Journal of Spiritual Formation and Soul Care* 12 (2020) 262–84.

Calhoun, Adele. *Spiritual Disciplines Handbook: Practices that Transforms Us.* 2nd ed. Downers Grove, IL: InterVarsity, 2015.

Calhoun, Lawrence, and Richard Tedeschi, eds. *Handbook of Posttraumatic Growth: Research and Practice.* Mahwah: Earlbaum, 2006.

———. *Posttraumatic Growth in Clinical Practice.* New York: Routledge, 2013.

Callaway, Kutter, and William Whitney. *Theology for Psychology and Counseling: Invitation to Holistic Christian Practice.* Grand Rapids: Baker Academic, 2022.

Captari, Laura, et al. "Integrating Religion and Spirituality into Psychotherapy: A Comprehensive Meta-Analysis." *Journal of Clinical Psychology* 74 (2018) 1938–51.

Carter, John, and Bruce Narramore. *The Integration of Psychology and Theology.* Grand Rapids: Zondervan, 1979.

Cashwell, Craig, and Scott J. Young, eds. *Integrating Spirituality and Religion into Counseling: A Guide to Competent Practice.* 3rd ed. Alexandria: American Counseling Association, 2020.

Castonguay, Louis, et al., eds. *Principles of Change: How Psychotherapists Implement Research in Practice.* New York: Oxford University Press, 2019.

Chan, Simon. Introduction to the Special Theme: Pentecostalism and Spiritual Formation. *Journal of Spiritual Formation and Soul Care* 13 (2020) 39–43.

Chandler, Diane, ed. *The Holy Spirit and Christian Formation: Multidisciplinary Perspectives.* Cham, Switzerland: Palgrave MacMillan, 2016.

Chapelle, Wayne. "A Series of Progressive Legal and Ethical Decision-Making Steps for Using Christian Spiritual Interventions in Psychotherapy." *Journal of Psychology and Theology* 28 (2000) 43–53.

Chase, Steven. *The Tree of Life: Models of Christian Prayer.* Grand Rapids: Baker Academic, 2005.

Coe, John. "Beyond Relationality to Union: Musings Toward a Pneumadynamic Approach to Personality and Psychotherapy." *Journal of Psychology and Christianity* 18 (1999) 109–128.

———. "Musings on the Dark Night of the Soul: Insights from St. John of the Cross on a Developmental Spirituality." *Journal of Psychology and Theology* 28 (2000) 293–307.

Coe, John, and Todd Hall. *Psychology in the Spirit: Contours of a Transformational Psychology.* Downers Grove, IL: IVP Academic, 2010.

Coe, John, and Kyle Strobel, eds. *Embracing Contemplation: Reclaiming a Christian Spiritual Practice*. Downers Grove, IL: IVP Academic, 2019.

Cole, Graham. *He Who Gives Life: The Doctrine of the Holy Spirit*. Wheaton, IL: Crossway, 2007.

Collicut, Joanna. *The Psychology of Christian Character Formation*. London: SCM, 2015.

Collins, Gary. *Christian Counseling: A Comprehensive Guide*. 3rd ed. Edited by Gary Collins. Nashville: Thomas Nelson, 2007.

———. *How to be a People Helper*. Santa Ana, CA: Vision House, 1976.

Comer, John. *The Ruthless Elimination of Hurry*. Colorado Springs: WaterBrook, 2019.

Cooper, John. *Body, Soul and Life Everlasting: Biblical Anthropology and the Monism-Dualism Debate*. Grand Rapids: Eerdmans, 1989.

Corcoran, Kevin. *Rethinking Human Nature: A Christian Materialist Alternative to the Soul*. Grand Rapids: Baker Academic, 2006.

Cortez, Marc. *Christological Anthropology in Historical Perspective: Ancient and Contemporary Approaches to Theological Anthropology*. Grand Rapids: Zondervan, 2016.

———. *Resourcing Theological Anthropology: A Constructive Account of Humanity in the Light of Christ*. Grand Rapids: Zondervan, 2017.

Crabb, Larry. *Effective Biblical Counseling*. Grand Rapids: Zondervan, 1977.

———. *The PAPA Prayer: The Prayer You've Never Prayed*. Brentwood, TN: Integrity, 2006.

———. *66 Love Letters: A Conversation with God that Invites You into His Story*. Nashville: Thomas Nelson, 2009.

———. *Soultalk: The Language God Longs for Us to Speak*. Brentwood, TN: Integrity, 2003.

———. *Understanding People: Deep Longings for Relationship*. Grand Rapids: Zondervan, 1987.

———. *Waiting for Heaven: Freedom from the Incurable Addiction to Self*. Larger Story, 2020.

Crisp, Oliver, and Fred Sanders, eds. *The Christian Doctrine of Humanity: Explorations in Constructive Dogmatics*. Grand Rapids: Zondervan, 2018.

———, eds. *The Third Person of the Trinity: Explorations in Constructive Dogmatics*. Grand Rapids: Zondervan Academic, 2020.

Crisp, Thomas, et al., eds. *Neuroscience and the Soul: The Human Person in Philosophy, Science, and Theology*. Grand Rapids: Eerdmans, 2016.

Decker, Edward. "The Holy Spirit in Counseling: A Review of Christian Counseling Journal Articles 1985–1999." *Journal of Psychology and Christianity* 21 (2002) 21–28.

Deere, Jack. *Surprised by the Power of the Spirit*. Grand Rapids: Zondervan, 1993.

———. *Surprised by the Voice of God*. Grand Rapids: Zondervan, 1996.

Dodds, Lois. "The Role of the Holy Spirit in Personality Growth and Change." *Journal of Psychology and Christianity* 18 (1999) 129–139.

Dueck, Alvin. "Babel, Esperanto, Shibboleths, and Pentecost: Can We Talk?" *Journal of Psychology and Christianity* 21 (2002) 72–80.

Dueck, Alvin, and Kevin Reimer. *A Peaceable Psychology: Christian Therapy in a World of Many Cultures.* Grand Rapids: Brazos, 2009.

Eck, Brian. "An Exploration of the Therapeutic Use of Spiritual Disciplines in Clinical Practice." *Journal of Psychology and Christianity* 21 (2002) 266–280.

———. "Integrating the Integrators: An Organizing Framework for a Multifaceted Process of Integration." *Journal of Psychology and Christianity* 15 (1996) 101–15.

Egan, Harvey. "Christian Apophatic and Kataphatic Mysticisms." *Theological Studies* 39 (1978) 399–426.

Entwistle, David. *Integrative Approaches to Psychology and Christianity.* 4th ed. Eugene, OR: Cascade, 2021.

Evans, C. Stephen. "The Blessings of Mental Anguish." *Christianity Today* 30 (1986) 26–29.

Exline, Julie. "Religious and Spiritual Struggles." In *APA Handbook of Psychology, Religion, and Spirituality: Volume 1. Context, Theory, and Research,* edited by Kenneth Pargament et al., 459–75. Washington, DC: American Psychological Association, 2013.

Farris, Joshua. *An Introduction to Theological Anthropology: Humans, Both Creaturely and Divine.* Grand Rapids: Baker Academic, 2020.

Fee, Gordon. *God's Empowering Presence: The Holy Spirit in the Letters of Paul.* Peabody, MA: Hendrickson, 1994.

———. "On Getting the Spirit Back into Spirituality." In *Life in the Spirit: Spiritual Formation in Theological Perspective* edited by Jeffrey Greenman and George Kalantzis, 36–44. Downers Grove, IL: IVP Academic, 2010.

Finney, John, and H. Newton Malony. "Contemplative Prayer and Its Use in Psychotherapy: A Theoretical Model." *Journal of Psychology and Theology* 13 (1985) 172–81.

———. "Empirical Studies of Christian Prayer: A Review of the Literature." *Journal of Psychology and Theology* 13 (1985) 104–15.

———. "An Empirical Study of Contemplative Prayer as an Adjunct to Psychotherapy." *Journal of Psychology and Theology* 13 (1985) 284–90.

Flynn, Mike and Doug Gregg. *Inner Healing.* Downers Grove, IL: InterVarsity, 1993.

Ford, Kristy, and Fernando Garzon. "Research Note: A Randomized Investigation of Evangelical Christian Accomodative Mindfulness." *Spirituality in Clinical Practice* 4 (2017) 92–99.

Foster, Richard. *Celebration of Discipline.* San Francisco: Harper & Row, 1978.

———. *Celebration of Discipline: The Path to Spiritual Growth,* special anniversary edition. New York: HarperOne, 2018.

———. *Prayer: Finding Your Heart's True Home.* San Francisco: HarperSanFrancisco, 1992.

Fox, Jesse, et al. "The Opiate of the Masses: Measuring Spiritual Bypass and Its Relationship to Spirituality, Religion, Mindfulness, Psychological Distress, and Personality." *Spirituality in Clinical Practice* 4 (2017) 274–87.

Fox, Jesse, et al. "Religious Commitment, Spirituality, and Attitudes Toward God as Related to Psychological and Medical Help-Seeking: The Role of Spiritual Bypass." *Spirituality in Clinical Practice* 7 (2020) 178–96.

Frank, Jerome. "Therapeutic Components Shared by all Psychotherapies." In *Psychotherapy Research and Behavior Change,* Master Lecture Series, Volume 1, edited by John Harvey and Marjorie Parks, 5–37. Washington, DC: American Psychological Association, 1982.

Garzon, Fernando. "Christian Devotional Meditation for Anxiety." In *Evidence-Based Practices for Christian Counseling and Psychotherapy,* edited by Everett Worthington Jr. et al., 59–78. Downers Grove, IL: IVP Academic, 2013.

———. "Interventions that Apply Scripture in Psychotherapy." *Journal of Psychology and Theology* 33 (2005) 113–21.

Garzon, Fernando, and Lori Burkett. "Healing of Memories: Models, Research, Future Directions." *Journal of Psychology and Christianity* 21 (2002) 42–49.

Garzon, Fernando, and Kristy Ford. "Adapting Mindfulness for Conservative Christians." *Journal of Psychology and Christianity* 35 (2016) 263–68.

Gass, Cartlon. "Orthodox Christian Values Related to Psychotherapy and Mental Health." *Journal of Psychology and Theology* 12 (1984) 230–37.

Gaultiere, Bill, and Kristi Gaultiere. *Journey of the Soul: A Practical Guide to Emotional and Spiritual Growth.* Grand Rapids: Revell, 2021.

Gilbert, Marvin, and Raymond Brock, eds. *The Holy Spirit and Counseling, Volume 1: Theology and Theory.* Peabody, MA: Hendrickson, 1985.

———. *The Holy Spirit and Counseling, Volume 2: Principles and Practice.* Peabody, MA: Hendrickson, 1988.

Gill, Carman, and Robert Freund, eds. *Spirituality and Religion in Counseling: Competency-Based Strategies for Ethical Practice.* New York: Routledge, 2018.

Green, Joel. *Body, Soul, and Human Life: The Nature of Humanity in the Bible.* Grand Rapids: Baker Academic, 2008.

Green, Joel, and Stuart Palmer, eds. *In Search of the Soul: Four Views of the Mind-Body Problem.* Downers Grove, IL: InterVarsity, 2005.

Greenman, Jeffrey. "Spiritual Formation in Theological Perspective: Classic Issues, Contemporary Challenges." In *Life in the Spirit: Spiritual Formation in Theological Perspective,* edited by Jeffery Greenman and George Kalantzis, 23–35. Downers Grove, IL: IVP Academic, 2010.

Greenman, Jeffery, and George Kalantzis, eds. *Life in the Spirit: Spiritual Formation in Theological Perspective.* Downers Grove, IL: IVP Academic, 2010.

Greggo, Stephen, and Timothy Sisemore, eds. *Counseling and Christianity: Five Approaches.* Downers Grove, IL: IVP Academic, 2012.

Grounds, Vernon. *Emotional Problems and the Gospel*. Grand Rapids: Zondervan, 1976.

Grudem, Wayne. *Systematic Theology: An Introduction to Biblical Doctrine*. 2nd ed. Grand Rapids: Zondervan, 2020.

Habets, Myk. *The Progressive Mystery: Tracing the Elusive Spirit in Scripture and Tradition*. Bellingham: Lexham, 2019.

Hall, M. Elizabeth, and Todd Hall. "Integration in the Therapy Room: An Overview of the Literature." *Journal of Psychology and Theology* 25 (1997) 86–101.

Hall, Todd, and M. Elizabeth Hall. *Relational Spirituality: A Psychological-Theological Paradigm for Transformation*. Downers Grove, IL: IVP Academic, 2021.

Hathaway, William. "Clinical Use of Explicit Religious Approaches: Christian Role Integration Issues." *Journal of Psychology and Christianity* 28 (2009) 105–12.

————. "Spiritual Gift Inventories: Validity and Function." *Journal of Psychology and Christianity* 37 (2018) 205–16.

Hathaway, William, and Mark Yarhouse. *The Integration of Psychology and Christianity: A Domain-Based Approach*. Downers Grove, IL: IVP Academic, 2021.

Hayes, Steven, et al. "Acceptance and Commitment Therapy: Model, Processes, and Outcomes." *Behaviour Research and Therapy* 44 (2006) 1–25.

Hayford, Jack. "Spirit-Formed in Purity and Power." *Spectrum* 6 (2005) 5–6.

Helgeson, Vicki, et al. "A Meta-Analytic Review of Benefit Finding and Growth." *Journal of Consulting and Clinical Psychology* 74 (2006) 797–816.

Hoffman, Marie. *Toward Mutual Recognition: Relational Psychoanalysis and the Christian Narrative*. New York: Routledge, 2011.

Hoffman, Lowell, and Brad Strawn. "Normative Thoughts, Normative Feelings, Normative Actions: A Protestant, Relational Psychoanalytic Reply to E. Christian Brugger and the Faculty of IPS." *Journal of Psychology and Theology* 37 (2009) 125–33.

Holeman, Virginia. *Theology for Better Counseling: Trinitarian Reflections for Healing and Formation*. Downers Grove, IL: IVP Academic, 2012.

Hook, Joshua, et al. "Empirically Supported Religious and Spiritual Therapies." *Journal of Clinical Psychology* 66 (2010) 46–72.

Hook, Joshua, et al. "Religion and Spirituality." In *Psychotherapy Relationships that Work. Volume 2: Evidence-Based Therapist Responsiveness,* edited by John Norcross and Bruce Wampold, 212–63. New York: Oxford University Press, 2019.

Horton, Michael. *Rediscovering the Holy Spirit: God's Perfecting Presence in Creation, Redemption, and Everyday Life*. Grand Rapids: Zondervan, 2017.

Houston, James. *The Transforming Friendship: A Guide to Prayer*. Oxford: Lion, 1989.

Hunsinger, Deborah. *Pray Without Ceasing: Revitalizing Pastoral Care*. Grand Rapids: Eerdmans, 2006.

Ingram, John. "Psychological Aspects of the Filling of the Holy Spirit: A Preliminary Model of Post-Redemptive Personality Functioning." *Journal of Psychology and Theology* 24 (1996) 104–13.

Jeeves, Malcolm, and Warren Brown. *Neuroscience, Psychology, and Religion: Illusions, Delusions, and Realities about Human Nature.* West Conshohocken: Templeton, 2009.

Johnson, Cedric. "Religious Resources in Psychotherapy." In *Psychotherapy in Christian Perspective,* edited by David Benner, 31–36. Grand Rapids: Baker Academic, 1987.

Johnson, Eric. "Christ, the Lord of Psychology." *Journal of Psychology and Theology* 25 (1997) 11–27.

———. *Foundations for Soul Care: A Christian Psychology Proposal.* Downers Grove, IL: IVP Academic, 2007.

———. *God and Soul Care: The Therapeutic Resources of the Christian Faith.* Downers Grove, IL: IVP Academic, 2017.

———, ed. *Psychology and Christianity: Five Views.* Downers Grove, IL: IVP Academic, 2010.

Jones, Russell. *Spirit in Session: Working with your Client's Spirituality (and Your Own) in Psychotherapy.* West Conshohocken: Templeton, 2019.

Jones, Tonya, et al. "Christian Accomodative Mindfulness in the Clinical Treatment of Shame, Depression, and Anxiety: Results of an N-of-1 Time-Series Study." *Spirituality in Clinical Practice.* 2021. Advance Online Publication.

Karkkainen, Veli-Matti. *Pneumatology: The Holy Spirit in Ecumenical, International, and Contextual Perspective.* 2nd ed. Grand Rapids: Baker Academic, 2018.

Kilner, John. *Dignity and Destiny: Humanity in the Image of God.* Grand Rapids: Eerdmans, 2015.

Knabb, Joshua. *Acceptance and Commitment Therapy for Christian Clients: A Faith-Based Workbook.* New York: Routledge, 2017.

———. *Christian Meditation in Clinical Practice: A Four-Step Model and Workbook for Therapists and Clients.* Downers Grove, IL: IVP Academic, 2021.

———. *Faith-Based ACT for Christian Clients: An Integrative Treatment Approach.* New York: Routledge, 2016.

Knabb, Joshua, and Thomas Frederick. *Contemplative Prayer for Christians with Chronic Worry: An Eight-Week Program.* New York: Routledge, 2017.

Knabb, Joshua, et al. "Christian Meditation for Repetitive Negative Thinking: A Multisite Randomized Trial Examining the Effects of a 4-Week Preventative Program." *Spirituality in Clinical Practice* 7 (2020) 34–50.

Knabb, Joshua, et al. *Christian Psychotherapy in Context: Theoretical and Empirical Explorations in Faith-Based Mental Health.* New York: Routledge, 2019.

Knabb, Joshua, et al. "Introduction to the Special Issue: Meditation, Prayer, and Contemplation in the Christian Tradition: Towards the Operationalization and Clinical Application of Christian Practices in Psychotherapy and Counseling." *Journal of Psychology and Christianity* 39 (2020) 5–11.

Knabb, J., and Veola Vasquez. "A Randomized Controlled Trial of a 2-Week Internet-Based Contemplative Prayer Program for Christians with Daily Stress." *Spirituality in Clinical Practice* 5 (2018) 37–53.

Knabb, Joshua, et al. "'Set your Minds on Things Above': Shifting from Trauma-Based Ruminations to Ruminating on God." *Mental Health, Religion and Culture* 22 (2019) 384–99.

Knabb, Joshua, et al. "Surrendering to God's Providence: A Three-Part Study on Providence-Focused Therapy for Recurrent Worry (PFT-RW)." *Psychology of Religion and Spirituality* 9 (2017) 180–96.

Knabb, Joshua, et al. "'Unknowing' in the 21st Century: Humble Detachment for Christians with Repetitive Negative Thinking." *Spirituality in Clinical Practice* 5 (2018) 170–87.

Kraft, Charles. *Deep Wounds, Deep Healing.* Ann Arbor, MI: Vine, 1993.

Kruis, John. *Quick Scripture Reference for Counseling.* 4th ed. Grand Rapids: Baker Academic, 2013.

Kunst, Jennifer, and Siang-Yang Tan. "Psychotherapy as 'Work in the Spirit': Thinking Theologically about Psychotherapy." *Journal of Psychology and Theology* 24 (1996) 284–91.

Ladd, Kevin, and Bernard Spilka. "Inward, Outward, Upward: Cognitive Aspects of Prayer." *Journal for the Scientific Study of Religion* 41 (2002) 475–84.

———. "Inward, Outward, Upward Prayer: Scale Reliability and Validation." *Journal for the Scientific Study of Religion* 45 (2006) 233–51.

Lambert, Heath. *A Theology of Biblical Counseling.* Grand Rapids: Zondervan, 2016.

Lambert, Michael, ed. *Bergin and Garfield's Handbook of Psychotherapy and Behavior Change.* 6th ed. Hoboken: Wiley, 2013.

LaPine, Matthew. *The Logic of the Body: Retrieving Theological Psychology.* Bellingham, WA: Lexham, 2021.

Lazarus, Arnold. *The Practice of Multimodal Therapy Updated Edition.* Baltimore: Johns Hopkins University Press, 1989.

Lee, Cameron. *Integration as Integrity: The Christian Therapist as Peacemaker.* Eugene, OR: Cascade, 2020.

Lee, Johnathan. *The Importance of Inner Healing and Deliverance for Effective Discipleship.* Eugene, OR: Wipf & Stock, 2019.

Levering, Matthew. *Engaging the Doctrine of the Holy Spirit: Love and Gift in the Trinity and the Church.* Grand Rapids: Baker Academic, 2016.

Levison, John. *A Boundless God: The Spirit According to the Old Testament.* Grand Rapids: Baker Academic, 2020.

———. *Filled with the Spirit.* Grand Rapids: Eerdmans, 2009.

———. *Inspired: The Holy Spirit and the Mind of Faith.* Grand Rapids: Eerdmans, 2013.

————. *An Unconventional God: The Spirit According to Jesus.* Grand Rapids: Baker Academic, 2020.

Lints, Richard, et al., eds. *Personal Identity in Theological Perspective.* Grand Rapids: Eerdmans, 2006.

Lovinger, Robert. *Working with Religious Issues in Therapy.* New York: Jason Aronson, 1984.

MacNutt, Francis. *Deliverance from Evil Spirits: A Practical Manual.* Grand Rapids: Chosen, 1995.

Malony, H. Newton. "The Clinical Assessment of Optimal Religious Functioning." *Review of Religious Research* 30 (1988) 2–17.

————. "Inner Healing." In *Psychotherapy in Christian Perspective,* edited by David Benner, 171–79. Grand Rapids: Baker Academic, 1987.

————. *Integration Musings: Thoughts on Being a Christian Professional.* 2nd ed. Pasadena, CA: Integration, 1995.

Mangelsdorf, Judith, et al. "Does Growth Require Suffering? A Systematic Review and Meta-Analysis on Genuine Posttraumatic and Postecstatic Growth." *Psychological Bulletin* 145 (2019) 302–38.

Marks, Isaac. "Behavioral Psychotherapy of Adult Neurosis." In *Handbook of Psychotherapy and Behavior Change: An Empirical Analysis,* edited by Sol Garfield and Allen Bergin, 493–547. New York: Wiley, 1978.

McCullough, Michael, and David Larson. "Prayer." In *Integrating Spirituality into Treatment,* edited by William Miller, 85–110. Washington, DC: American Psychological Association, 1999.

McKnight, Scot. *Open to the Spirit: God in Us, God with Us, God Transforming Us.* New York: WaterBrook, 2018.

McMinn, Mark. *Psychology, Theology, and Spirituality in Christian Counseling.* Wheaton, IL: Tyndale, 1996.

McMinn, Mark, and Clark Campbell. *Integrative Psychotherapy: Toward a Comprehensive Christian Approach.* Downers Grove, IL: IVP Academic, 2007.

McMinn, Mark and Barrett McRay. "Spiritual Disciplines and the Practice of Integration: Possibilities and the Challenges for Christian Psychologists." *Journal of Psychology and Theology* 25 (1997) 102–10.

Miller, Keith. *Quick Scripture Reference for Counseling Men.* Grand Rapids: Baker Academic, 2014.

Miller, Keith, and Patricia Miller. *Quick Scripture Reference for Counseling Couples.* Grand Rapids: Baker Academic, 2017.

————. *Quick Scripture Reference for Counseling Youth.* Updated and revised ed. Grand Rapids: Baker Academic, 2014.

Miller, Patricia. *Quick Scripture Reference for Counseling Women.* Updated and revised ed. Grand Rapids: Baker Academic, 2013.

Miller, William, and Janet C'de Baca. *Quantum Change: When Epiphanies and Sudden Insights Transform Ordinary Lives.* New York: Guilford, 2001.

Moltmann, Jürgen. *The Source of Life: The Holy Spirit and the Theology of Life.* Minneapolis: Fortress, 1997.

Monroe, Philip. "Guidelines for the Effective Use of the Bible in Counseling." *Edification: Journal of the Society for Christian Psychology* 2 (2008) 53–61.

Moon, Gary, and David Benner, eds. *Spiritual Direction and the Care of Souls.* Downers Grove, IL: InterVarsity, 2004.

Murphy, Nancy. "Nonreductive Physicalism: Philosophical Challenges." In *Personal Identity in Theological Perspective,* edited by Richard Lints et al., 95–117. Grand Rapids: Eerdmans, 2006.

Murray-Swank, Aaron, and Nichole Murray-Swank. "Spiritual and Religious Problems: Integrating Theory and Clinical Practice." In *APA Handbook of Psychology, Religion, and Spirituality: Volume 2. An Applied Psychology of Religion and Spirituality,* edited by Kenneth Pargament et al., 421–37. Washington, DC: American Psychological Association, 2013.

Neff, Megan, and Mark McMinn. *Embodying Integration: A Fresh Look at Christianity in the Therapy Room.* Downers Grove, IL: IVP Academic, 2020.

Nelson, Alan, and William Wilson. "The Ethics of Sharing Religious Faith in Psychotherapy." *Journal of Psychology and Theology* 12 (1984) 15–23.

Nieuwsma, Jason, et al., eds. *ACT for Clergy and Pastoral Counselors: Using Acceptance and Commitment Therapy to Bridge Psychological and Spiritual Care.* Oakland: Context, 2016.

Norcross, John, and Marvin Goldfried, eds. *Handbook of Psychotherapy Integration.* 3rd ed. New York: Oxford University Press, 2019.

Norcross, John, and Michael Lambert, eds. *Psychotherapy Relationships that Work. Volume 1: Evidence-Based Therapist Contributions.* 3rd ed. New York: Oxford University Press, 2019.

Norcross, John, and Bruce Wampold, eds. *Psychotherapy Relationships that Work. Volume 2: Evidence-Based Therapist Responsiveness.* 3rd ed. New York: Oxford University Press, 2019.

Oman, Doug, and Joseph Driskill. "Holy Name Repetition as a Spiritual Exercise and Therapeutic Technique." *Journal of Psychology and Christianity* 22 (2003) 5–19.

Ortberg, John. *The Life You've Always Wanted: Spiritual Disciplines for Ordinary People.* Exp. ed. Grand Rapids: Zondervan, 2002.

———. *Soulkeeping: Caring for the Most Important Part of You.* Grand Rapids: Zondervan, 2014.

Outler, Albert. "The Wesleyan Quadrilateral in Wesley." *Wesleyan Theological Journal* 20 (1985) 7–18.

Packer, James. *Keep in Step with the Spirit: Finding Fullness in Our Walk with God.* Rev. ed. Grand Rapids: Baker, 2005.

Pargament, Kenneth. *Spiritually Integrated Psychotherapy: Understanding and Addressing the Sacred.* New York: Guilford, 2007.

Pargament, Kenneth, et al. "Spiritual Struggle: A Phenomenon of Interest to Psychology and Religion." In *Judeo-Christian Perspectives on Psychology: Human Nature, Motivation, and Change,* edited by William Miller and

Harold Delaney, 245–68. Washington, DC: American Psychological Association, 2005.

Pargament, Kenneth, et al., eds. *APA Handbook of Psychology, Religion, and Spirituality—Vol. 2. An Applied Psychology of Religion and Spirituality.* Washington, DC: American Psychological Association, 2013.

Park, Crystal, and Vicki Helgeson. "Introduction to the Special Section: Growth Following Highly Stressful Events—Current Status and Future Directions." *Journal of Consulting and Clinical Psychology* 74 (2006) 791–96.

Park, Crystal. "Making Sense of the Meaning Literature: An Integrative Review of Meaning Making and its Effects on Adjustment to Stressful Life Events." *Psychological Bulletin* 136 (2010) 257–301.

Park, Crystal, et al. *Trauma, Meaning, and Spirituality: Translating Research into Clinical Practice.* Washington, DC: American Psychological Association, 2017.

Parker, Stephen. "Winnicott's Object Relations Theory and the Work of the Holy Spirit." *Journal of Psychology and Theology* 36 (2008) 285–93.

Parks-Stamm, Elizabeth, et al. "The Impact of Prayer Direction on Emotional and Cognitive Responses to Personal Problems." *Psychology of Religion and Spirituality* 12 (2020) 471–74.

Payne, I. Reed, et al. "A Review of Attempts to Integrate Spiritual and Standard Psychotherapy Techniques." *Journal of Psychotherapy Integration* 2 (1992) 171–92.

Payne, Leanne. *Restoring the Christian Soul: Overcoming Barriers to Completion in Christ Through Healing Prayer.* Grand Rapids: Baker Academic, 1991.

Peck, M. Scott. *Further Along the Road Less Traveled.* New York: Simon & Shuster, 1993.

Pinnock, Clark. *Flame of Love: A Theology of the Holy Spirit.* Downers Grove, IL: InterVarsity, 1996.

Plante, Thomas. *Spiritual Practices in Psychotherapy: Thirteen Tools for Enhancing Psychological Health.* Washington, DC: American Psychological Association, 2009.

Plummer, Robert. "Are the Spiritual Disciplines of "Silence and Solitude" Really Biblical?" *Journal of Spiritual Formation and Soul Care* 2 (2009) 101–12.

Poloma, Margaret, and Brian Pendleton. "The Effects of Prayer and Prayer Experiences on Measures of General Well-Being." *Journal of Psychology and Theology* 19 (1991) 71–83.

———. "Exploring Types of Prayer and Quality of Life: A Research Note." *Review of Religious Research* 31 (1989) 46–53.

Porter, Steven. "A Reply to the Respondents of 'Theology as Queen and Psychology as Handmaid.'" *Journal of Psychology and Christianity* 29 (2010) 33–40.

———. "Theology as Queen and Psychology as Handmaid: The Authority of Theology in Integrative Endeavors." *Journal of Psychology and Christianity* 29 (2010) 3–14.

Propst, L. Rebecca, et al. "Comparative Efficacy of Religious and Nonreligious Cognitive-Behavioral Therapy for the Treatment of Clinical Depression in Religious Individuals." *Journal of Consulting and Clinical Psychology* 60 (1992) 94–103.

Puchalska-Wasyl, Malgorzata, and Beata Zarzycka. "Prayer and Internal Dialogical Activity: How do they Predict Well-Being?" *Psychology of Religion and Spirituality* 12 (2020) 417–27.

Puffer, Keith. "Essential Biblical Assumptions about Human Nature: A Modest Proposal." *Journal of Psychology and Christianity* 26 (2007) 45–56.

Pugh, John. *Christian Formation Counseling: The Work of the Holy Spirit in the Human Race.* Mustang: Tate & Enterprises, 2008.

Reissman, Frank. "The 'Helper Therapy' Principle." *Social Work* 10 (1965) 27–32.

Richards, P. Scott, and Allen Bergin, eds. *Casebook for a Spiritual Strategy for Counseling and Psychotherapy.* Washington, DC: American Psychological Association, 2004.

—————, eds. *Handbook of Psychotherapy and Religious Diversity.* 2nd ed. Washington, DC: American Psychological Association, 2014.

—————. *A Spiritual Strategy for Counseling and Psychotherapy.* 2nd ed. Washington, DC: American Psychological Association, 2005.

Richardson, Rick. *Experiencing Healing Prayer.* Downers Grove, IL: InterVarsity, 2005.

Rogers, Steven. "Where the Moment Meets the Transcendent: Using the Process as a Spiritual Intervention in Object Relations Psychotherapy." *Journal of Psychology and Christianity* 26 (2007) 151–58.

Rosales, Aaron, and Siang-Yang Tan. "Acceptance and Commitment Therapy (ACT): Empirical Evidence and Clinical Applications from a Christian Perspective." *Journal of Psychology and Christianity* 35 (2016) 269–75.

Rosales, Aaron, and Siang-Yang Tan. "Mindfulness-Based Cognitive Therapy (MBCT): Empirical Evidence and Clinical Applications from a Christian Perspective." *Journal of Psychology and Christianity* 36 (2017) 76–82.

Rose, Elizabeth, et al. "Spiritual Issues in Counseling: Clients' Beliefs and Preferences." *Journal of Counseling Psychology* 48 (2001) 61–71.

Sandage, Steven, and Jeannine Brown. *Relational Integration of Psychology and Theology: Theory, Research, and Practice.* New York: Routledge, 2018.

Sandage, Steven, et al. *Relational Spirituality in Psychotherapy: Healing Suffering and Promoting Growth.* Washington, DC: American Psychological Association, 2020.

Sanders, Randolph, ed. *Christian Counseling Ethics: A Handbook for Therapists, Pastors, and Counselors.* 2nd ed. Downers Grove, IL: IVP Academic, 2013.

Sbanotto, Elisabeth, et al. *Skills for Effective Counseling: A Faith-Based Approach.* Downers Grove, IL: IVP Academic, 2016.

Seamands, David. *Healing of Memories.* Wheaton: Victor, 1985.

Sears, Richard, and Alison Niblick, eds. *Perspectives on Spirituality and Religion in Psychotherapy.* Sarasota: Professional Resource, 2014.

Shigematsu, Ken. *Survival Guide for the Soul: How to Flourish Spiritually in a World that Pressures us to Achieve.* Grand Rapids: Zondervan, 2018.

Smith, Edward. *Healing Life's Hurts Through Theophostic Prayer.* Campbellsville, KY: New Creation, 2002/2005.

Sorenson, Randall. "The Tenth Leper." *Journal of Psychology and Theology* 24 (1996) 197–211.

Sorenson, Randall, et al. "National Collaborative Research on how Students Learn Integration: Final Report." *Journal of Psychology and Christianity* 23 (2004) 355–65.

Sperry, Len. *Spirituality in Clinical Practice: Theory and Practice of Spiritually Oriented Psychotherapy.* 2nd ed. New York: Routledge, 2011.

Sperry, Len, and Edward Shafranske, eds. *Spiritually Oriented Psychotherapy.* Washington, DC: American Psychological Association, 2005.

Spilka, Bernard, and Kevin Ladd. *The Psychology of Prayer: A Scientific Approach.* New York: Guilford, 2013.

Stewart-Sicking, et al. *Bringing Religion and Spirituality into Therapy: A Process-Based Model for Pluralistic Practice.* New York: Routledge, 2020.

Storms, Sam. *Practicing the Power: Welcoming the Gifts of the Holy Spirit in your Life.* Grand Rapids: Zondervan, 2017.

Strawn, Brad. "Clinical Integrative Practice (CIP)." *Journal of Psychology and Theology* 48 (2020) 237–38.

Strawn, Brad, and Warren Brown. *Enhancing Christian Life: How Extended Cognition Augments Religious Community.* Downers Grove, IL: IVP Academic, 2020.

Strawn, Brad, et al. "Learning Clinical Integration: A Case Study Approach." *Journal of Psychology and Theology* 46 (2018) 85–97.

Strawn, Brad, et al. "Tradition-Based Integration: Illuminating the Stories and Practices that Shape our Integrative Imagination." *Journal of Psychology and Christianity* 33 (2014) 300–310.

Strobel, Kyle, and John Coe. *Where Prayer Becomes Real: How Honesty with God Transforms Your Soul.* Grand Rapids: Baker, 2021.

Sutton, Geoffrey. *Counseling and Psychotherapy with Pentecostal and Charismatic Christians: Culture and Research / Assessment and Practice.* Springfield: Sunflower, 2021.

Swindoll, Chuck. "Helping and the Holy Spirit." *Christianity Counseling Today* 2 (1994) 16–19.

Tan, Siang-Yang. "Addressing Religion and Spirituality from a Cognitive Behavioral Perspective." In *APA Handbook of Psychology, Religion and Spirituality: Volume 2. An Applied Psychology of Religion and Spirituality,* edited by Kenneth Pargament et al., 169–87. Washington, DC: American Psychological Association, 2013.

———. "Beyond Resilience, Posttraumatic Growth, and Self-Care: A Biblical Perspective on Suffering and Christian Spiritual Formation." In *Psychology and Spiritual Formation in Dialogue: Moral and Spiritual Change in*

Christian Perspective, edited by Thomas Crisp et al., 104–22. Downers Grove, IL: IVP Academic, 2019.

———. "Cognitive-Behavior Therapy: A Biblical Approach and Critique." *Journal of Psychology and Theology* 15 (1987) 103–12.

———. *Counseling and Psychotherapy: A Christian Perspective.* 2nd ed. Grand Rapids: Baker Academic, 2022.

———. "Cultural Issues in Spirit-Filled Psychotherapy." *Journal of Psychology and Christianity* 18 (1999) 164–76.

———. "Developing Integration Skills: The Role of Clinical Supervision." *Journal of Psychology and Theology* 37 (2009) 54–61.

———. "Faith in Psychology and Counseling: Being Spirit-Filled Servants of Jesus Christ." *Edification: Journal of the Society for Christian Psychology* 2 (2008) 63–68.

———. *Full Service: Moving Beyond Self-Serve Christianity to Total Servanthood.* Grand Rapids: Baker, 2006.

———. "The Holy Spirit and Counseling Ministries." *Christian Journal of Psychology and Counseling* 7 (1992) 8–11.

———. "The Holy Spirit and Positive Psychology in Spiritual Formation." In *Tending Soul, Mind, and Body: The Art and Science of Spiritual Formation,* edited by Gerald Heistand and Todd Wilson, 36–48. Downers Grove, IL: IVP Academic, 2019.

———. "Holy Spirit: Role in Counseling." In *Baker Encyclopedia of Psychology and Counseling,* edited by David Benner and Peter Hill, 568–69. Grand Rapids: Baker Academic, 1999.

———. "Inner Healing Prayer." *Christian Counseling Today* 11 (2003) 20–22.

———. "Integrating Spiritual Direction into Psychotherapy: Ethical Issues and Guidelines." *Journal of Psychology and Theology* 31 (2003) 14–23.

———. "Integration and Beyond: Principled, Professional, and Personal." In *Journal of Psychology and Christianity* 20 (2001) 18–28.

———. "Intrapersonal Integration: The Servant's Spirituality." *Journal of Psychology and Christianity* 6 (1987) 34–39.

———. "Is Suffering Necessary for Growth? Posttraumatic Growth and Postecstatic Growth: Empirical Evidence and Clinical Applications from a Christian Perspective." *Journal of Psychology and Christianity* 38 (2019) 283–87.

———. *Lay Counseling: Equipping Christians for a Helping Ministry.* Grand Rapids: Zondervan, 1991.

———. "Mindfulness and Acceptance-Based Cognitive Behavioral Therapies: Empirical Evidence and Clinical Applications from a Christian Perspective." *Journal of Psychology and Christianity* 30 (2011) 243–49.

———. "My Integration Journey: Reflections of a Christian Psychologist and Pastor." In *Integrating Faith and Psychology: Twelve Psychologists Tell Their Stories,* edited by Glendon Moriarty, 69–92. Downers Grove, IL: IVP Academic, 2010.

———. "My Pilgrimage as a Christian Psychologist." In *Storying Ourselves: A Narrative Perspective on Christians in Psychology*, edited by John Lee, 131–53. Grand Rapids: Baker, 1993.

———. "Principled, Professional, and Personal Integration and Beyond: Further Reflections on the Past and Future." *Journal of Psychology and Theology* 40 (2012) 146–49.

———. "Psychology Collaborating with the Church: A Pastor-Psychologist's Perspective and Personal Experience." In *Psychology and the Church*, edited by Mark McMinn and Amy Dominguez, 49–55. Hauppauge: Nova Science, 2005.

———. "Religion in Clinical Practice: Implicit and Explicit Integration." In *Religion and the Clinical Practice of Psychology*, edited by Edward Shafranske, 365–87. Washington, DC: American Psychological Association, 1996.

———. *Shepherding God's People: A Guide to Faithful and Fruitful Pastoral Ministry*. Grand Rapids: Baker Academic, 2019.

———. "Use of Prayer and Scripture in Cognitive-Behavioral Therapy." *Journal of Psychology and Christianity* 26 (2007) 101–11.

Tan, Siang-Yang, and Brad Johnson. "Spiritually Oriented Cognitive-Behavioral Therapy." In *Spiritually Oriented Psychotherapy*, edited by Len Sperry and Edward Shafranske, 77–103. Washington, DC: American Psychological Association, 2005.

Tan, Siang-Yang, and Douglas Gregg. *Disciplines of the Holy Spirit*. Grand Rapids: Zondervan, 1997.

Tan, Siang-Yang, and Eric Scalise. *Lay Counseling: Equipping Christians for a Helping Ministry*. Revised and updated ed. Grand Rapids: Zondervan, 2016.

Tan, Siang-Yang, and John Ortberg. *Coping with Depression*. Revised ed. Grand Rapids: Baker, 2004.

Tang, Alex. "Not just for Monks: Spiritual Disciplines are for Anyone Who wants to Love God and Others More." *Asian Beacon* 40 (2008) 8–9.

Terrell, Jeffrey. "A Discussion of Intentional Incarnational Integration in Relational Psychodynamic Psychotherapy." *Journal of Psychology and Christianity* 26 (2007) 159–65.

Thiselton, Anthony. *The Holy Spirit—In Biblical Teaching, through the Centuries, and Today*. Grand Rapids: Eerdmans, 2013.

Thomas, Gary. *Authentic Faith: The Power of a Fire-Tested Life*. Grand Rapids: Zondervan, 2002.

Thomas, John, ed. *Counseling Techniques: A Comprehensive Resource for Christian Counselors*. Grand Rapids: Zondervan, 2018.

Thomas, John, and Lisa Sosin. *Therapeutic Expedition: Equipping the Christian Counselor for the Journey*. Nashville: B & H Academic, 2011.

Tolin, David, et al. "Empirically Supported Treatment: Recommendations for a New Model." *Clinical Psychology: Science and Practice* 22 (2015) 317–38.

Trammel, Regina. "Effectiveness of an MP3 Christian Mindfulness Intervention on Mindfulness and Perceived Stress." *Mental Health, Religion and Culture* 21 (2017) 500–514.

Trammel, Regina, et al. "Religiously Oriented Mindfulness for Social Workers: Effects on Mindfulness, Heart Rate Variability, and Personal Burnout." *Journal of Religion and Spirituality in Social Work: Social Thought* 40 (2020) 19–38.

Trammel, Regina, and John Trent. *A Counselor's Guide to Christian Mindfulness: Engaging the Mind, Body, and Soul in Biblical Practices and Therapies.* Grand Rapids: Zondervan, 2021.

Vasquez, Veola, and Gregory Jensen. "Practicing the Jesus Prayer: Implications for Psychological and Spiritual Well-Being." *Journal of Psychology and Christianity* 39 (2020) 65–74.

Vining, John. *Pentecostal Caregivers: Anointed to Heal.* East Rockaway, NY: Cummings & Hathaway, 1995.

———. *Spirit-Centered Counseling: A Pneumascriptive Approach.* East Rockaway, NY: Cummings & Hathaway, 1995.

Vining, John, and Edward Decker, eds. *Soul Care: A Pentecostal-Charismatic Perspective.* East Rockaway, NY: Cummings & Hathaway, 1996.

Wade, Nathaniel, et al. "Effectiveness of Religiously Tailored Interventions in Christian Therapy." *Psychotherapy Research* 17 (2007) 91–105.

Wagner, C. Peter. *Your Spiritual Gifts can Help Your Church Grow.* Updated and expanded. Ventura: Regal, 2005.

Walker, Donald et al. "Therapists' Use of Religious and Spiritual Interventions in Christian Counseling: A Preliminary Report." *Counseling and Values* 49 (2005) 107–19.

Walker, Donald, et al. "Use of Religious and Spiritual Interventions by Trainees in APA-Accredited Christian Clinical Programs." *Mental Health, Religion and Culture* 11 (2008) 623–33.

Walker, Donald, et al., eds. *Spiritually Oriented Therapy for Trauma.* Washington, DC: American Psychological Association, 2014.

Walker, Donald, and William Hathaway, eds. *Spiritual Interventions in Child and Adolescent Psychotherapy.* Washington, DC: American Psychological Association, 2013.

Wampold, Bruce, and Zac Imel. *The Great Psychotherapy Debate: The Evidence for What Makes Psychotherapy Work.* 2nd ed. Mahwah, NJ: Erlbaum, 2015.

Wang, David, and Siang-Yang Tan. "Dialectical Behavior Therapy (DBT): Empirical Evidence and Clinical Applications from a Christian Perspective." *Journal of Psychology and Christianity* 35 (2016) 68–76.

Wardle, Terry. *Healing Care, Healing Prayer.* Orange: New Leaf, 2001.

Warren, Tish. *Liturgy of the Ordinary: Sacred Practices in Everyday Life.* Downers Grove, IL: InterVarsity, 2016.

Watson, Terri. *Developing Clinicians of Character: A Christian Integrative Approach to Clinical Supervision.* Downers Grove, IL: IVP Academic, 2018.

Weld, Chet, and Karen Eriksen. "Christian Clients' Preferences Regarding Prayer as a Counseling Intervention." _Journal of Psychology and Theology_ 35 (2007) 328–41.

White, Frances. "Spiritual and Religious Issues in Therapy." In _Psychotherapy in Christian Perspective_, edited by David Benner, 37–46. Grand Rapids: Baker Academic, 1987.

White, Kristen. "Conceptualizing Therapy as a Spiritual Discipline." _Journal of Psychology and Christianity_ 39 (2020) 91–103.

Whitney, Donald. _Spiritual Disciplines for the Christian Life_. Revised and updated ed. Colorado Springs: NavPress, 2014.

Whittington, Brandon, and Steven Scher. "Prayer and Subjective Well-Being: An Examination of Six Different Types of Prayer." _The International Journal for the Psychology of Religion_ 20 (2010) 59–68.

Wilder, E. James, et al. "A Christian Multi-Modal Approach to Therapy Utilizing Inner Healing Prayer: The Life Model." _Journal of Psychology and Christianity_ 39 (2020) 49–64.

Willard, Dallas. _The Divine Conspiracy: Rediscovering Our Hidden Life in God_. New York: HarperSanFrancisco, 1998.

———. _The Great Omission: Reclaiming Jesus' Essential Teachings on Discipleship_. San Francisco: HarperSanFrancisco, 2006.

———. _The Spirit of the Disciplines_. San Francisco: Harper & Row, 1988.

———. "Spirituality: Going Beyond the Limits." _Christian Counseling Today_ 4 (1996) 16–20.

Winnicot, Donald W. _The Maturational Processes and the Facilitating Environment_. New York: International Universities Press, 1966.

———. _Playing and Reality_. New York: Basic, 1971.

Wong, Paul, et al., eds. _The Positive Psychology of Meaning and Spirituality_. Abbortsford, BC: INPM, 2007.

Worthington, Everett, Jr., et al., eds. _Evidence-Based Practices for Christian Counseling and Psychotherapy_. Downers Grove, IL: IVP Academic, 2013.

Wright, Ronald, et al. "Tradition-Based Integration." In _Christianity and Psychoanalysis: A New Conversation_, edited by Earl Bland and Brad Strawn, 37–54. Downers Grove, IL: IVP Academic, 2014.

Yong, Amos. _Spirit of Love: A Trinitarian Theology of Grace_. Waco, TX: Baylor University Press, 2012.

Printed in the USA
CPSIA information can be obtained
at www.ICGtesting.com
LVHW091249090124
768527LV00004B/26